What every Christian needs to know—

about *Temptation* and *Putting sin to death*

What every Christian needs to know—

about *Temptation*
and *Putting sin to death*

An abridgement and rewrite of two works by John
Owen, on temptation and the mortification of sin. The
full works are available from the Banner of Truth
Trust, Edinburgh, EH12 6EL

Prepared by A. Swanson

© Grace Publications Trust
7 Arlington Way
London EC1R 1XA
England

Joint Managing Editors
J.P. Arthur MA
H.J. Appleby

First published 1998

Reprinted 2007

ISBN 978-0-946462-47-6

Distributed by Evangelical Press
Grange Close
Faverdale North Industrial Estate
Darlington
Co. Durham DL3 0PH
England

Printed and bound in Great Britain by Biddles Ltd,
King's Lynn, Norfolk

Cover design L.L. Evans

Part one

Temptation

A practical guide to recognising its approach and resisting its power and purpose

Contents

Chapter   **Page**

*Owen's Chapter 3 has been divided here into 3, 4, 5, to make for ease in reading.

1.
The Saviour's warning against temptation

The disciples were feeling secure, although danger was just around the corner! It was then that the Lord gave this warning, 'Watch and pray, so that you will not fall into temptation,' (Matthew 26:41; Mark 14:38; & Luke 22:46). Every disciple of Christ needs the same warning. This warning contains three very basic lessons that every Christian needs to learn well.

1) Every Christian must constantly be on guard against temptation.
2) To 'Fall into temptation' is to experience temptation in its most powerful and dangerous form.
3) To avoid being harmed by such an experience of temptation the believer must learn to 'watch and pray'.

Before we are ready for any of these lessons we must examine the basic teaching of the Bible on temptation.

In the Bible we see two different types of temptation. There is a good kind of temptation that God uses; there is an evil kind of temptation that Satan uses. Temptation is like a knife. It can be used for a good or a bad purpose: it may either cut a man's meat or his throat.

1) The good kind of temptation that God uses.

Sometimes the Bible uses the word temptation to mean a trial or testing. (Note: Modern translations often use the word 'test' or 'trial' rather than 'temptation' where God's activity is concerned.) Abraham was tested by God (Genesis 22:1ff) and in one way or another all believers are subject to trials and testings (for example James 1:2 and 1 Peter 1:6).

There are two important points to note about such trials.

Note 1 - The purpose of God in sending trials.

a) Trials help the believer to know about his spiritual health. Sometimes the experience of a trial will show the believer spiritual graces that God is producing in his life. God's trial of Abraham displayed the strength of his faith. Sometimes a trial will show the believer evils in his heart that he had never known about. God tried Hezekiah and revealed to him the pride of his heart (2 Chronicles 32:31). Sometimes believers need to be encouraged by seeing spiritual graces at work in their lives. At other times believers need to be humbled by learning the hidden evils of their hearts. God meets both these needs through the use of suitable trials.

b) Trials help the believer to know more about God.
i) It is God alone who can keep the believer from falling into sin. Until we are tempted we think we can handle temptation in our own strength. Peter thought he would never deny his Lord. Temptation showed him that he would (Matthew 26:33-35, 69-75).

ii) When we have learned our weakness and the power of temptation we are ready to discover the power of God's grace. This is the great lesson the Apostle Paul was taught through his 'thorn in the flesh' (See 2 Corinthians 12:7-10).

10

Note 2 - God has many ways of testing his people.

God tests every believer in a very personal way. Here are three examples of the methods God sometimes uses to test his people.

a) He tests them by giving them duties that are beyond their own resources. The Apostle Paul refers to such testing when he writes, 'We were under great pressure, far beyond our ability to endure' (2 Corinthians 1:8). This was a test that the Lord used to teach Paul, 'not to rely on himself but on God, who raises the dead' (2 Corinthians 1:9). Believers must not be surprised or dismayed if God gives them a task that seems beyond them. In this way God tests believers, to show them whether their faith in God's power is strong or weak.

b) He tests believers by permitting them to suffer for their faith. Sometimes the suffering is very severe, even to the point of death. Such suffering is a trial that most believers dread. Yet many believers have found unexpected strength given them to be tortured or even to die for Christ's sake. All Christians are called to sufferings of one kind or another (Philippians 1:29, 1 Peter 2:21). The Apostle Peter calls such sufferings 'the trial of your faith' (1 Peter 1:7, A.V.).

c) He tests believers by allowing them to meet false teachers or false teaching. God tests the believer's loyalty and love for himself in this way. Deuteronomy 13:1ff gives a good example of this kind of testing.

These are three examples of the variety of methods God uses to test his people. This type of testing that God uses is always intended for the good of his people. We are now ready to turn to the type of temptation that Satan uses.

11

2) The evil kind of temptation that Satan uses.

Both types of temptation contain the idea of trial. Temptation is always a trial! The point to remember about the type of temptation Satan uses is its purpose. Temptation of this type is a trial designed to lead a person into sin. God is *never* the author of this type of temptation (James 1:13). It is this type of temptation that the Lord was warning his disciples about. It is this type of temptation which we shall study.

The Bible teaches that there are three major causes of this type of temptation. Sometimes these causes work together, sometimes separately.

Firstly - The devil is a tempter. Twice in the New Testament the devil, or Satan, is called 'the tempter' (Matthew 4:3, 1 Thessalonians 3:5). Sometimes the devil will tempt a believer to sin by putting evil or blasphemous thoughts into his mind. Sometimes there is the temptation to doubt the reality of God or the truth of his Word. This temptation often comes through evil thoughts injected into the mind by the devil. Temptations of this kind are called 'the flaming arrows of the evil one' (Ephesians 6:16). The believer is not guilty of sin because he has these thoughts. The believer is only guilty of sin if he believes these thoughts.

More often the devil will tempt by making use of two other ways:-

Secondly - The world (including worldly people) is a tempter. A fisherman uses the bait of a tasty worm to catch a fish. In the same way the devil often uses the bait of some attraction of the world to persuade a person to sin. When the devil tempted Christ, he used the kingdoms of this world as his bait. It was a servant girl who tempted Peter to deny his Lord (Matthew 26:69). The world with all its things and people is a constant source of temptation to believers.

12

Thirdly - The flesh (i.e. selfish desire) is a tempter. Sometimes the devil works through a person's desires in order to tempt him. The devil tempted Judas to betray his Lord by using both the help of the world (i.e. the Pharisees and thirty pieces of silver, Matthew 26:14-16) and the covetous nature of Judas himself. In the words of James, 'Each one is tempted when, by his own evil desire, he is dragged away and enticed' (James 1:14).

The kind of temptation used by the devil is always an attempt to persuade a person to sin. Such temptation may aim at persuading a person to sin in any or all of the following ways: neglecting his God-given duty; entertaining evil in his heart; allowing Satan to draw evil out of his heart; allowing Satan to divert him in any way from communion with God; failing to give God constant, equal, universal obedience to all that he requires (including the manner in which that obedience is given).

We are now ready to give some brief thought to the first of the three basic lessons listed at the start of this chapter.

1) Every Christian must constantly be on guard against temptation. We will illustrate the dangers of temptation by Satan under two points:

a) The great harm that Satan's temptation can bring to a believer. A major aim of temptation is to lead a person into sin. It may be a sin of doing what God forbids. It may be a sin of not doing what God commands. It may be a sin of the flesh that can be seen by others. It may be a sin of the mind, that only God can see. Whatever the sin may be, we must never forget that the aim of such temptation is to harm the spiritual health of the believer.

b) The great varieties of temptation that Satan seeks to use against a believer. Anything that can hinder us in doing the will of God must be seen as a temptation. It may be something within us (i.e. some evil desire) or any thing or person in the world. Anything that provokes or encourages a person to sin is a kind of temptation. Almost any desire a person may have could prove to be a source of temptation. It is not sinful in itself to want such things as an easy life, friends, a good standard of living, a good reputation (the list is endless!). These things, however, can all become a dangerous source of temptation that is hard to resist. Christians need to learn to fear temptations from such sources. They need to fear such temptations as much as they would fear temptations that lead to open and scandalous sin. If we fail to do this we are nearer the brink of ruin than we realise!

2.
Temptation — handle with care!

In the main part of this chapter we will focus attention upon the danger of temptation by considering the meaning of two phrases we find in the New Testament:-

1) 'To enter into temptation' (Matthew 26:41, A.V.)
2) 'The hour of temptation' (Revelation 3:10, A.V.)

1) 'To enter into temptation'.
What did Jesus mean by the words 'enter into temptation'? We will begin to answer this by looking at two very common wrong answers.

a) To 'enter into temptation' simply means 'to be tempted'. This answer is wrong because God nowhere promises absolute freedom from temptation. Jesus would not teach us to pray for something that God would not give. Some temptations may be avoided, but in this life it is impossible to escape completely from temptation. 'To enter into temptation' is a more dangerous experience than mere temptation.

b) To 'enter into temptation' means to be conquered by temptation. This answer is also wrong because a person may 'enter into temptation' and yet not be defeated by temptation. It was a period of 'entering into temptation' that Joseph experienced (see Genesis 39:6-12), but Joseph came out of it triumphant.

In 1 Timothy 6:9 Paul likens a 'fall into temptation' to being caught in a trap. The main idea of being caught in a trap is that you cannot easily escape from it. In 1 Corinthians 10:13, Paul uses the expression, 'no temptation has seized you'. This expression is meant to illustrate the power of temptation and the difficulty of escaping it. In 2 Peter 2:9 Peter highlights for us the power of certain temptations. We can only escape from such temptations with the help of the superior power of God.

From these references we draw the conclusion that to 'enter into temptation' means to experience to an usual degree the captivating power of temptation. Sometimes temptation is like a salesman knocking at the door. It can be ignored or told to go away and it does. At other times temptation cannot be dealt with so easily. At such times temptation is like a salesman with his foot in the door. Not only is this salesman determined to get a sale for his goods but also his goods are very attractive. As long as temptation simply 'knocks at the door' we are free to ignore it. When temptation gets past 'the door' and enters into 'the room of our heart', then we 'enter into temptation'.

When a person 'enters into temptation' he experiences the power of temptation from two sources.

c) Satan's power acts in a special way from outside the person. Satan comes with more determination and power than usual to tempt the person into sin. Sometimes he tempts by intimidation: that is 'sin or else! Deny Christ or lose your life'. Sometimes he aims to tempt by offering something that will be desirable to the person; for example, 'all this I will give you, if you will bow down and worship me' (Matthew 4:9).

d) The power of indwelling sin acts in a special way from within. Indwelling sin may be likened to a traitor who lives in the heart of every person. This traitor takes the side of the tempter and tries to encourage the one who is tempted to give way to temptation. In such a temptation the believer may cry to God for deliverance again and again and yet not be delivered. The temptation continues to make its demands. Such temptations usually occur in one or other of the following circumstances:

i) When Satan gains special permission from God, for reasons best known to God himself, to bring the believer to 'enter into temptation, (2 Samuel 24:1, cf. 1 Chronicles 21:1; Job 1:12, 2:6; Luke 22:31).

ii) When a man's evil desires are provided with a favourable opportunity and a highly desirable means of being fulfilled. Such was the case with David as recorded in 2 Samuel 11.

2) 'The Hour of temptation'.

Whenever one or other of these circumstances occurs, a man enters into temptation or, as it is called in Revelation 3:10, 'the hour of temptation'. At such a time the captivating power of temptation reaches the height of its strength. It is at this time that temptation is most dangerous and likely to overcome any resistance offered. Many temptations never reach this point and are conquered without great difficulty. When the same temptation occurs at 'the hour of temptation', it has a new strength. Unless special grace is given, it will conquer the soul and lead it into sin. Probably David had temptations to adultery or murder in his younger days (e.g. the case of Nabal, see 1 Samuel 25) but it was not until his 'hour of temptation' that these particular temptations came with a strength and urgency that overwhelmed him (2 Samuel 11).

17

Unless a person is specially prepared for an hour like this he will certainly fall under such temptation. There are two further questions about 'the hour of temptation' that must be considered.

a) What are the common means used to bring temptation to its hour?

i) When Satan aims at making a person enter into temptation he will frequently and persistently present the particular temptation to the mind. He seeks to dull our minds to the sinfulness of the temptation by going on and on. Our mind may be horrified at the first temptation, but as the temptation persists, this horror weakens and the temptation appears less evil than at first.

ii) If a Christian sees his brother fall into sin, he should respond by hating the sin, feeling pity for his fallen state and praying for his deliverance. If he does not respond in this way Satan will use this weakness as a means of bringing him into the same temptation himself. When Hymenaeus and Philetus wandered away from the truth, others fell in the same way (2 Timothy 2:17,18).

iii) The evil of a temptation may be hidden by the introduction of other considerations (often considerations which are good in themselves). For example, the temptation to the Galatians to fall from the purity of the gospel promised with it freedom from persecution. The desire to be free from persecution actually added power to the temptation to fall from the purity of the gospel.

b) How can we know we have come to the hour of temptation?

i) When Satan brings a person to the hour of temptation, it can be known by its restless pressure. It is as if Satan knows that it is 'now or never' and he will give the soul no rest. In a war, if the enemy gains an advantage over his opponent, he redoubles his efforts. In the same way, when Satan has weakened a Christian's resolve to resist him, he uses all his powers and cunning to conquer and persuade him to sin. Whenever temptation presses on all sides (from within and without) to gain the consent of the will to sin, we may be sure that 'the hour of temptation' has come.

ii) Whenever temptation combines the power of fear with the power of attraction, temptation has come to its hour. The whole strength of temptation consists in the combination of these two powers. Each of these powers, on its own, is often enough to persuade a person to sin. Working together they seldom fail. We find both these powers at work in the case of David's murder of Uriah. There was fear of Uriah's revenge on his wife (not to mention the possibility of Uriah seeking revenge on David) and the fear of his sin being made public. That was united to the attraction of the present enjoyment of sinning with Bathsheba. Whenever a person is aware of feeling the force of these two powers seeking to persuade him to sin, temptation has come to its hour.

We are now ready to turn, very briefly, to the subject that will occupy our interest for the rest of this book.

To avoid being harmed by such an experience of temptation the believer must learn to 'watch and pray'

To watch means to be on our guard, to take heed, to consider all ways and means that could be used by the enemy of our souls to overwhelm us by temptation. This will involve a consistent and diligent watch over our souls using all the means that God has given for this purpose. In particular, it will include the lifelong study of our enemy's schemes and our own strengths and weaknesses that Satan would exploit to entangle us in sin.

In addition to watching, we must pray. This is the means by which we can receive God's help to watch as we should and so resist Satan's advances. All the work of faith to keep our soul from temptation is summed up in these two duties - 'watch and pray'.

19

3.
Why be so serious about temptation?

We have laid our foundation. We come now to the great purpose of this study:

It is the great duty of every believer to make every effort, using the means Christ has given, not to fall into temptation

Why is this duty so important? In this chapter we will think of three reasons that the Bible gives us.

Reason 1:
The Lord Jesus gave us a pattern for daily prayer. In this pattern one request is, 'lead us not into temptation, but deliver us from evil' (Matthew 6:13, A.V.). This petition may be paraphrased, 'so deal with us that we may be powerfully delivered from that evil which attends our entering into temptation'. Our blessed Saviour knows how dangerous temptation is and how we need the help of God to keep us from falling into temptation. We trust in the wisdom, love and care of Jesus for his people. He emphasises this duty; we must take it seriously.

Reason 2:

The Lord Jesus promised a great reward to the church of Philadelphia (Revelation 3:10). That reward was deliverance from a testing trial that would come upon the whole world. Do you desire this blessing? Then you will take seriously the duty that Christ has appointed as a means to preserve us in or from such trial.

Reason 3:

When we consider the horrifying consequences that have been the result of men (both bad and good men) entering into temptation, wisdom demands that we take this duty very seriously. These horrifying consequences can be illustrated from the experience of two distinct classes of people:

a) People who appear to be, but are not, genuine Christians.

These people are described by the Lord Jesus in his parable of the sower as 'rocky ground hearers'. They 'receive the word with joy when they hear it, but they have no root. They believe for a while, but in the time of testing they fall away' (Luke 8:13). In every age there are people like this. They seem to make a good start in the Christian life, but sooner or later they fall in a time of temptation and abandon their Christian profession. These people are also pictured by the Lord Jesus as being like a 'foolish man who built his house on sand'. What does this house do? It shelters these people for a while, but when the testing of a stormy day comes it will fall with a great crash (Matthew 7:26,27).

We see that Judas followed the Lord Jesus for three years. No one but Jesus could see the difference between Judas and the rest of the twelve. No sooner did Judas enter into temptation than he fell away, never to be restored. Demas identified himself with the Apostle Paul until the love of the world overcame him and he deserted Paul (2 Timothy 4:10). En-

21

trance into temptation for such people is an entrance into apostasy. In many cases the apostasy is plain for all to see; in others it will only become plain at the day of judgement.

b) People who are true believers
The Bible gives many illustrations of the horrifying consequences of genuine saints entering into temptation. We must limit ourselves to a few examples:

Adam: Adam was created in the image of God, with a holy nature, and therefore not subject to the sinful desires of a fallen nature. Yet even he was overcome by temptation as soon as he entered it. As a result, he was lost and ruined, and so was the whole human race. If a man in such ideal conditions as Adam can fall so easily, what hope is there for the rest of the human race? We have to contend not only with the devil, as Adam did, but also with a world under God's curse and all the sinful desires of a fallen nature.

Abraham: Abraham, the father of the faithful, twice entered into the same temptation. Fears about his wife's safety tempted him to lie. God was dishonoured and Abraham doubtless experienced sorrow and remorse (Genesis 12:12, 13; 20:2).

David: David, 'the man after God's own heart', entered into the temptation to lust after another woman. He fell into the sins of adultery and sinful scheming that involved other people in his sin. He even made a plan that led to the murder of a good man.

Many others: The temptation and falls of many others such as Noah, Lot, Hezekiah and Peter are recorded for our instruction. They give us painful evidence of how easily saints can fall into grievous sin as the result of entering into temptation. In the

22

light of such illustrations each one of us will do well to pray: *'O Lord, if such illustrious and mighty saints can fall so miserably when they enter into temptation, how can I stand in such a day? O keep me that I enter not such temptation!'*

God has given us many warnings and many examples of others who have fallen into sin when they were tempted. In spite of this some Christians go boldly into temptation's way. What extreme foolishness!

4.
The power of temptation

Reason 4:
If we consider our own weakness we will find plenty of reasons
to take the duty of 'watching and praying' very seriously.

Our weakness can be seen from two standpoints:

a) We have no power or strength of our own to withstand 'the hour of temptation'

A major part of every man's weakness is a misguided confidence in his own strength. Peter's confidence in himself
(Matthew 26:33) was certainly his weakness. Most people are
the same. We never manage to do anything as well as we think
we can. What is worse, sinful desire is like a traitor in our
hearts. It is ready to betray us to the enemy. This is the reason
why we must never flatter ourselves that we have the strength
to stand in the hour of temptation. We may pride ourselves in
thinking that there are certain things we will never do. We
forget that the heart is never the same under temptation as it is
before we enter into temptation. Little did Peter think he would
deny his Lord as soon as someone questioned him. When the
hour of temptation came, all Peter's resolutions were forgotten, all love to Christ was temporarily buried and the temptation united with Peter's fear and completely overcame him.

Trusting in our own strength is such a common failure that

we will be wise to examine it a little more closely. What are we trusting in?

i) In general
We are trusting in our own hearts. Many an unbeliever flatters himself that he has a good heart but the Bible says, 'The heart of the wicked is of little value' (Proverbs 10:20). It is the heart that temptation will battle against. How can a worthless heart stand before a mighty temptation? The true believer who trusts in his own heart is no better, because the Bible says,
'He that trusteth in his own heart is a fool' (Proverbs 28:26 A.V.). Peter was a true believer, but he proved himself to be a fool when he trusted in his own heart. The Bible also says, 'The heart is deceitful above all things' (Jeremiah 17:9, A.V.). Dare we trust in that which is 'deceitful above all things'?

ii) To be more specific
We are trusting that the heart has strong enough motivation to avoid being overcome by temptation. Can these motivations be strong enough? Think of a few examples.

a) Love of honour in the world
The reputation and esteem a man has gained over the years of a faithful Christian life and witness are important. Some people think they are a sufficiently powerful motivation to stand firm in the hour of temptation. These people think they would rather die than give up the reputation they have gained in the church of God. Alas, however, this is not a strong enough motivation to keep a man from falling into sin. This did not keep Judas, Hymenaeus or Philetus (2 Timothy 2:17). Nor will it keep anyone else from falling in the hour of temptation.

b) The fear of shame, loss or reproach
Some people are confident that the sheer fear of bringing shame or reproach upon themselves or the cause of Christ is a

strong enough incentive to stand firm in the hour of temptation. This can only apply to temptation that involves open, observable sin. Those who depend upon this motivation will soon find in the day of temptation that it does not have the power they thought it had.

c) The fear of a disturbed conscience and the fear of hell

The fear of a wounded conscience and going to hell are thoughts we would do well to consider frequently. However, these fears, on their own, are no guarantee that we shall stand firm in the hour of temptation. There are at least three reasons why these considerations will fail to preserve us:

i) Sometimes the peace of conscience that a person wants to preserve is a false peace. After David had sinned with Bathsheba and before the prophet Nathan came, David was at peace. It was a false peace. Worse still, many an unbeliever thinks that he has peace with God, but it is a false peace. Just as a false peace will prove useless on the day of judgement, so it will prove useless in an hour of temptation.

ii) A true peace of conscience is valuable. However, by itself it will not be enough to preserve a person in the hour of temptation. The reason for this is that a deceitful heart is able to produce a variety of compelling reasons why it is not important to preserve peace of conscience. Here are two of them: 'Other believers have fallen and yet recovered their peace'. And, 'If I do lose my peace, it can be regained'. When the hour of temptation comes, these and many similar arguments will soon weary the soul into giving up its peace.

iii) To think that the desire to keep our peace of conscience is sufficient to preserve us in the hour of temptation is like a soldier thinking that as long as he wears a helmet he will not be injured in battle. Peace of conscience is a part of the armour needed to overcome temptation. However, if it is the only piece of armour used, temptation will soon find an unprotected target.

d) The wickedness of sinning against God

You may have a vivid awareness of the wickedness of sinning against God. That seems a strong protection against the hour of temptation. How can I sin against the God of my salvation? How can I wound my Saviour Jesus Christ who died for me? Again it has to be said that this protection on its own is not enough to preserve from sin in the hour of temptation. Every day produces sad evidence that this consideration alone will fail. Every time a child of God falls into sin, temptation has overcome this protection.

We have considered weakness from the standpoint of our lack of power. Now we must consider:

b) The power of temptation to darken the mind

The influence of drink affects a man's judgement (Hosea 4:11). Temptation has the power to impair a man's judgement in the same way. The god of this world blinds the minds of those who do not believe the gospel so that they cannot see the glory of Christ (2 Corinthians 4:4). In a very similar way every temptation takes away a man's clarity of understanding and judgement. Temptation exercises this power in a variety of ways, but we will only consider three of the most common:

i) Temptation can dominate a man's imagination and thought so much that he cannot think about anything else.

When a man is tempted there are many considerations that would bring relief, but temptation is so strong that it dominates his mind and imagination. He is unable to concentrate on the things that would save him. He is like a man who is dominated by a problem. There are many ways of working through the problem, but he is so preoccupied with the problem itself that he is blind to every possible solution.

ii) Temptation can use a man's desires and emotions to muddle his mind and hinder him from thinking clearly.
Whenever a person allows his desires or emotions to control his thinking, he will cease to think clearly. Temptation will often captivate a man's desires and emotions to such an extent that the man is no longer in control of his reason. Before he enters into a particular temptation he may see quite clearly that a certain course of action is wrong. However, when temptation comes to that man and works upon his desires or emotions, he no longer thinks clearly. Soon he is thinking of ways to justify or excuse his sinful actions.

iii) Temptation will provoke the evil desires of a man's heart to such an extent that these desires will rule the mind.
Sinful desire is like a fire. Temptation is the fuel that will make it blaze and go out of control. A man's reason will often persuade him to keep his sinful desires in check by reminding him of the consequences of what he wants to do. If the fire of temptation works on that sinful desire, reason no longer has the power to hold it in check. No one knows the violence and power of a sinful desire until it meets with a temptation specially suited to it. Even the best of men can be surprised and overwhelmed by the power of a sinful desire when it meets with a suitable temptation. Just think how quickly Peter's fear rushed him into denying his Lord. Dare you consider yourself strong when you have such a powerful enemy?

c) The power of communal temptation
In Revelation 3:10 the Lords speaks of a temptation ('hour of trial' N.I.V.) that was going to 'come upon the whole world to test those who live on the earth'. This 'hour of trial' came to test the careless professing Christians of that day. Satan came as a roaring lion to persecute them and as an angel of light to try to lead them astray. We must think about three aspects of this kind of trial:

i) This kind of trial is a judgement from God. God has two aims in it.

One is the punishment of the world which has despised his gospel. The other is the judgement of those who falsely profess to be Christians. This means that the trial has a special power so that it will accomplish the purpose of God. The Bible speaks of people 'who refuse to love the truth and so be saved', people who did not believe the truth but delighted in wickedness. In order to punish them, 'God sends them a powerful delusion so that they will believe the lie...' (2 Thessalonians 2:9-12). God has not changed. In his holy sovereignty he still sends such trials, and these are never in vain. God gives them a power that will accomplish what he desires.

ii) This kind of trial involves the temptation to follow the example of other professing Christians who have a reputation for being godly.

In times of increasing wickedness, the general standard of godliness amongst the people of God will drop. This decline will start with a few believers who begin to grow careless, worldly and negligent of Christian duty. These believers begin to question the old ways and feel free to follow their sinful desires. At first, other believers will condemn and maybe reprove them. However, after a while many more will conform to the example of these few believers. Before long it will be hard to find people who are truly godly.

This principle, 'a little yeast works through the whole batch of dough' (1 Corinthians 5:6; Galatians 5:9), needs to be taken seriously. All it needs is a few influential believers who continue in their spiritual declension and who justify it to others. Soon a multitude will follow their example. It is easier to follow a multitude to do evil than it is to stand out for what is right. The same principle holds true with regard to false teaching. What do you need to change the whole doctrinal stand-point of a church? All it needs is a few influential believers who continue to promote and justify false teaching. It will not be long before a multitude will follow them.

How few Christians realize the strength of the temptation to follow the example of others! In every age Christians must learn to put their confidence in the Word of God, not in godly men. If we are humble, we shall seriously consider the opinions and practices of those with a reputation for godliness. However, it is not necessary to follow their example if their opinions and practices are contrary to the Word of God.

iii) This kind of temptation usually includes strong reasons for following a multitude to evil.

In the previous point we noted that there is a strong temptation to follow the example of people who have a good reputation. Added to this, these leaders to evil give what appear to be very good reasons for the opinions they hold or the example they give. Are you ready to think for yourself? Or do you allow other people to think for you? If so, you will be easily led astray by other people's false conclusions.

For example, the New Testament undoubtedly gives very clear teaching on the liberty that Christians are given through Christ. Sadly, it is not difficult for some to pervert this teaching. Slowly but surely, the safeguards of God's holy law are removed and Christian liberty is turned into a licence to sin. If Christians saw, at the very start of the teaching, where it was going to take them, they would probably turn from it with horror.

It could well be that some of the teachers themselves do not know where their teaching is going to take them. At the start the deviation from truth seems small and insignificant. Without being aware of it, the teachers and their followers drift further and further from the truth until 'they exchange the truth of God for a lie' (Romans 1:25). For example, there is a growing number of professing Christians today who are prepared to tone down and nullify the Bible's condemnation of homosexual practices. This is an up-to-date illustration of this principle.

d) The power of personal temptation
We have already dealt in part with the power of temptation as it affects the individual under the heading 'The power of temptation to darken the mind'. Now we simply want to add two further points:

Firstly:
Why is the 'hour of temptation' so strong? There are two powers at work when we are tempted. One is the power of temptation from outside ourselves. The other is the sinful desire of the heart. In the 'hour of temptation' these two powers meet and each power strengthens the other. Because of the temptation, our sinful desires grow stronger; because our sinful desires have grown stronger, the power of temptation to cause us to fall grows yet stronger.

There are some people (Christians included) who once would never have thought of indulging in certain sinful practices. They are now indulging in them with little sense of shame or remorse. How has this come to pass? We can illustrate the process with a common example: the breakup of a Christian marriage through adultery. When these people marry they genuinely expect to remain faithful. But all around us we see adultery, even amongst Christians. How does this happen?

The answer lies in this principle of the power of temptation giving strength to the sinful desire for adultery. As the sinful desire is strengthened, so the power of temptation grows until the combined power of both persuades to committing the sin of adultery. This is not a sudden event. There was a process that took place, a process that went on for many years before the actual sin was committed. Generally, the process happens something like this. After some years of married life, one of the partners experiences the temptation to be unfaithful. This first temptation finds a response because it appeals to a sinful desire already in the heart.

The first temptation finds a response, but the soul partly resists. Maybe it is even shocked to find itself contemplating doing such a thing. The temptation is resisted. However, though the temptation is resisted, it has entered the soul and started its work of strengthening the sinful desire to that sin. Temptation feeds that desire in a variety of ways. So the desire grows. As a result the actual temptation grows in strength. After a while, the sinful desire has grown so strong that it only needs temptation to provide a suitable occasion, and the sin will be committed.

There is only one satisfactory way of resisting temptation. It is to deal directly with the sinful desires that temptation aims to strengthen. As soon as we become aware of a sinful desire, whether it be ambition, pride, worldliness, uncleanness or anything else, we must work at putting to death that desire. The choice is this: the sinful desire must die or the soul must die.

Secondly:

We must also consider that the work of temptation affects the whole soul and not just the sinful desire to which it appeals. We can illustrate this by returning to our previous example. When the first temptation to unfaithfulness comes to a Christian, his reason will tell him that this temptation must be resisted. However, once temptation has made its entrance into the soul it will also work on his reason. Reason should be governed by conscience and oppose temptation. However, it becomes governed by desire and favours temptation. As sinful desire grows stronger, it will, by one means or another, take the whole soul along with it.

Once again, we note a process taking place. At first the reason, directed by the voice of conscience, opposes the temptation. Once the temptation enters the soul, we find that

the reason is progressively working in favour of the temptation. In a little while the reason that previously could not
contemplate such sin is slowly but surely beginning to contemplate the pleasure this sin could bring. Step by step the reason
is enlisted to banish the dread and fear of sin. Finally, it is
encouraging and justifying the very sin that once it could not
contemplate. It is frightening to consider the power of temptation to pervert the use of reason for its own wicked ends.

Learn from your own experience

We should always learn from our own experience and that of
others. What does your past experience of temptation teach
you? Does it not teach you that temptation has defiled your
conscience, spoiled or stolen your peace, weakened you in
your obedience and hidden the smile of God from you?
Perhaps temptation has failed to persuade you to give way to
some sinful desire. Even then, has it not left its dirty imprint on
your soul and caused much turmoil? We all admit that we
seldom, if ever, come out of temptation without spiritual loss.
If this is your experience, can you ever willingly let yourself be
trapped by temptation? If you are enjoying liberty from temptation, take great care to avoid entering temptation again in
case something worse may happen to you.

Satan's aim in tempting men is always the same. In every
temptation the ultimate aim is to dishonour God and to ruin our
souls. Dare you treat temptation lightly or try to play with it
when you know what temptation is designed to do? Do you
really believe what temptation aims to do, both to God and
yourself? Then gratitude to God demands that you use the
means he has appointed to frustrate the aim of Satan in your
temptation.

5.
Is all this effort really necessary?

We have given many reasons why Christians should earnestly
try to avoid temptation. It should be clear to all that this is our
Christian duty. However, some people still raise objections
which may undermine our resolve.

First objection:
We are commanded to 'count it all joy when we fall into divers
temptations' (James 1:2 A.V.). So, why should we make every
effort to avoid temptation? There are two answers to this
question.

a) James is not suggesting that we rejoice in the actual temptations into which we fall. Nor is he suggesting that there is
anything wrong in making every effort to avoid temptation.
What he is saying is this: in God's providence we sometimes
have to face temptation. At these times we are to rejoice, not
in the temptation itself, but in the purpose of God in bringing
us into temptation (James 1:3,4).

b) As we noted in the opening chapter, the Bible uses the word
temptation in two senses. James himself uses the word in two
different senses (see 1:2 and cf. 1:13 - The N.I.V. uses 'trials'
v.2. and 'tempted' v.13 to bring out the difference). In the first

sense it is God who is using the temptation or trial and it is intended for a good purpose. In the second sense it has the idea of trying to persuade to sin. Only the devil tempts in this way. No one can rejoice that he is tempted to sin by the devil because the aim of such temptation is wholly evil. God designs trials for our good. This may give the devil an opportunity to tempt us to sin. We are to rejoice in the trial yet seek to avoid any temptation to sin that could come from it.

Second objection:

Jesus Christ himself was tempted, so how can it be evil for us to share a similar experience? In addition, surely Hebrews 2:17,18 suggests that this experience was advantageous in that it enabled him to be a merciful priest?

Answer:

It is true that Jesus Christ was tempted, but it is equally true that he did not wilfully go in the way of temptation. To do this, he said, was 'to tempt the Lord thy God' (Matthew 4:7 A.V.). He suffered temptation, but he knew no sin. He never sinned. When the prince of this world came to Christ, he had 'no hold on him' (John 14:30). It is very different with us. He has something in us; an ally in our sinful desires. We never come out of temptation as Christ did, pure and undefiled. It is impossible for us to escape temptation completely but we must do all we can to avoid being trapped and defiled by it.

Third objection:

God has made promises to keep us in temptation (e.g. 1 Corinthians 10:13; 2 Peter 2:9). So why should we strive to keep ourselves from entering into temptation?

Answer:

God has given precious promises. They are to encourage us in our struggle against temptation. To claim the promises as an excuse not to fight against temptation ourselves is to abuse God's promises. Notice the promise in 1 Corinthians 10:13. It follows the clear command, 'If you think you are standing firm, be careful that you do not fall'.

a) If we wilfully enter temptation, or if we neglect our duty and so enter into temptation, the promise is not for us. The promise is made to those who enter temptation in spite of all their efforts to avoid doing so. It is not an indiscriminate promise to us if we willingly enter temptation. In one of the devil's temptations of the Lord Jesus he tried to trap him into sin by twisting the Scriptures and leaving out the phrase 'all your ways' (Psalm 91:11). This phrase is important. Jesus was not deceived, because he knew that the promise of deliverance is to those who are in the ways of God. He also knew that to listen to the devil was not one of the ways of God. If we go willingly in a way of temptation we are leaving the ways of God. God's promises are for those who are in his ways, not for those who leave them.

b) A child of God knows that God's grace is sufficient to keep him from falling away from God. He knows he can never perish (John 10:28). This knowledge does not encourage him to be careless about temptation. A Christian will tremble at the dishonour to God, the scandal to the gospel and the spiritual darkness that will fill his soul if he should fall into sin. By contrast, anyone who simply avoids temptation only out of fear of hell is more in danger of going there than he realizes.

c) To enter temptation simply because you believe it will not damn you is the same as to 'go on sinning, so that grace may increase' (Romans 6:1,2). Imagine an owner of a ship who just purchased at great expense a cargo of costly merchandise. He would be a fool if he willingly allowed his ship to smash itself upon rocks simply because he believed he could swim to shore on a plank. As Christians we have greater blessings than costly merchandise. We have comfort, peace and joy; we can bring glory to God and honour the gospel. It is even greater madness for us to risk the loss of all this because we believe our souls will be safe in the end.

6.

Entrance into temptation — the symptoms

If a person wants to avoid entering into temptation, he needs to know the symptoms of such an experience.

1) When it is too late and sin has been committed.

This may seem to be stating the obvious but it needs to be said. Whenever a man falls into any sin, he may be sure that he arrived at that sin by way of entering into temptation. All sin is from temptation. There can be no sin without temptation (James 1:14, 15; Galatians 6:1). When they are overtaken by a sin many people repent of the sin yet fail to recognise that temptation was its cause. If you wish to conquer any sin, you must consider what is tempting you to that sin and aim at avoiding the temptation. Temptation is the root and sin is the bitter fruit of temptation. Too many people are aware of their sins but not of their temptations. Such people are displeased with the bitter fruit of sin but do not take any precautions to avoid the poisonous root of temptation. You never suddenly fall into sin without first entering into temptation.

The company of certain people can almost certainly lead to sinful thoughts, words or deeds (1 Corinthians 15:33), yet it is possible to enjoy that company and later mourn over the sin

resulting from it. Certain aims or ambitions (e.g.
1 Timothy 6:9) can cause the same effect. Yet people can
follow these without appreciating the sorrows of sin that will
result from following them.

2) The strength of temptation

As we noted in the first chapter, temptations have several
degrees. **When temptation is violent, or constantly repeated, giving the soul no rest, then we may be sure we have
entered into temptation.** A person's sinful desires have the
power to seduce that person to sin without any external
temptation (James 1:14), but this is not the same as entering
into temptation.

Sinful desires are like a stream flowing on its way to the sea,
and temptation is like a powerful wind that blows on that
stream. Think of such a stream and imagine an empty boat
being put into it. Sooner or later, according to the course and
speed of the stream, that boat will be carried to the sea. In the
same way, a person's sinful desires will sooner or later (apart
from the saving grace of God) carry him to the sea of his eternal
ruin. Returning to our illustration, suppose there are strong
winds blowing on the boat. Then the boat will be driven with
violence against every bank and rock, until it is broken in
pieces and swallowed up in the sea.

This illustration gives us two pictures of a sinful man. The
first is that of a man slowly but surely being carried to the sea
of his eternal ruin on the stream of his sinful desires. The
second shows the same man experiencing the strong wind of
temptation. This wind hurries the man into one sin after
another until — a total wreck — he arrives at his eternal ruin.

This illustration can be followed out in many examples
taken from the lives of saints who were preserved from eternal
ruin, yet entered into temptation and fell badly, to their shame.
Hezekiah had the root of pride in him always (a sinful desire

that would have damned him were it not for the grace of God). Yet it did not make him show off his treasure and riches until he fell into temptation through the arrival of the ambassadors from the king of Babylon (2 Kings 20:12-19; cf. 2 Chronicles 32:24-31). That same sinful root of pride can be seen in David. For many years he resisted his sinful desire to number the people, but fell to this desire when Satan stood up and provoked him to it (2 Samuel 24:1-10 cf. 1 Chronicles 21:1-8). Similar illustrations can be found in the lives of Abraham, Jonah and Peter, to name a few. Judas Iscariot gives us a fearful example of a man who was never a true saint. Judas was covetous from the beginning (John 12:6) yet he did not try to satisfy this sinful desire by betraying his master until the devil entered into him.

We all have sinful desires. Sometimes the pressing opportunity comes for these to be satisfied. When this happens we have entered into temptation.

3) Our attitude towards our temptation

A person can enter into temptation without being aware of any sinful desire being stirred up. An example of this is the situation when a person's heart begins secretly to like the temptation and is content to provide for it and give it an opportunity to grow in various ways — yet without committing obvious sin.

This is a very subtle form of temptation. An example will help us to detect it. A man begins to gain a reputation for godliness, wisdom, learning, etc. (things good in themselves). People praise him for that and he begins to enjoy it. His pride and ambition are affected by it. He now makes great efforts to improve his gifts and graces. But his motives are wrong; he is wanting to improve his reputation. He is entering into temptation. If he does not recognise and deal with it, this subtle temptation will quickly make him a slave to the sinful desire of wanting a good reputation.

Jehu is a good Old Testament example of such a man. He had come to recognize that he was gaining a reputation for zeal. Jonadab, a good and holy man, meets Jehu. 'Now' thinks Jehu, 'here is an opportunity to improve my reputation'. So he calls Jonadab to him and sets to work earnestly. The things he did were good in themselves but his motives were not good. He was following his desires. He had entered into temptation.

Those involved in the work of the ministry and preaching the gospel are particularly liable to fall into this kind of subtle temptation. Many things about such work can be the means of gaining a reputation and the esteem of good men. A man's general ability, his plainness, faithfulness, boldness, success, etc. may all become the way of improving his reputation. Do we ever begin secretly to like the temptation? Do we begin to do some good for the wrong reason? Then we are entering into temptation.

4) Whenever a man's sinful desires and temptations meet

Whenever a man finds himself in a situation where his sinful desires are being given the opportunity of being satisfied and he finds himself being encouraged to make the most of the opportunity, then that man has entered into temptation. It is almost impossible for a man to be given the opportunities, occasions or advantages most suited to his sinful desires without that man becoming trapped. When ambassadors came from the king of Babylon, Hezekiah's pride cast him into temptation. When Hezael became king of Syria (2 Kings 8:7-15; cf. 13:3, 22), his cruelty and ambition made him rage savagely against Israel. When the priests came with their pieces of silver, Judas's covetousness was instantly at work to sell his master (Luke 22:3-6).

Inflammable material must be kept away from fire. In the same way, it is important to keep away from those things which will stir up our sinful desires. Some men think they can play with snakes and not be bitten, touch wet paint and not get stained, play with fire and not be burned; but they are mistaken. Does your work, your way of life or the company you keep bring opportunities for satisfying your sinful desires? If so, you have entered into temptation. Only God knows how you will come out of it!

5) The poor state of a man's soul indicates that he has entered into temptation

Just as a man in poor physical health is more liable to disease, so a man in poor spiritual health is more liable to fall by temptation. To be more specific, whenever a man's spiritual life is weakened, that man has entered into temptation. He may at first be ignorant of the particular temptation that he has entered into. However, it will not be long before he finds, to his own grief and sorrow, what it is. To help us detect this particular entrance into temptation, we must consider the ways in which a man's spiritual life can be weakened. Neglect of, or a formal performance of, Christian duties always leads to the weakening of spiritual life. When a person can omit duties or content himself with a careless, lifeless performance of them (without the delight, joy or satisfaction to his soul that he once enjoyed), then that person is growing spiritually weak.

This is a certain rule: **If a Christian's heart grows cold, negligent, or formal in the worship of God, one temptation or another has started to work in his heart.** The love of the world, or pride, or uncleanness, or self-seeking, or malice and envy, or one thing or another has possessed his spirit. To borrow the words of Hosea 'His hair is sprinkled with grey, but he does not notice' (Hosea 7:9b). It is important to be aware that a Christian, especially for the sake of conscience, can go through all the motions of Christian worship, such as praying, reading and hearing preaching of God's Word, yet with a cold unaffected heart; there is no real life in the performance of these duties. The church at Sardis kept up the performance of religious duties. That is how it gained a reputation for being alive; but the Lord knew better and his verdict was, 'You are dead' or 'about to die' (Revelation 3:1,2).

There is such a closeness between the new nature and the duties of the worship of God (this closeness is wonderfully illustrated in Psalm 119) that they will not be kept apart unless some secret temptation makes the soul unhealthy. Therefore, if a Christian finds, by honest self-examination, that his 'spiritual pulse' is not what it should be — if he finds little relish in or desire for the things of God — he should conclude that he has entered temptation, even though the form of temptation is not yet clear. Such a Christian is in a dangerous spiritual condition. If he does not find and deal with the cause of his spiritual weakness, it is very unlikely he will escape from a great temptation to sin. God in his great mercy may prevent this. On the other hand he may chasten that Christian by withdrawing the awareness of his presence from him (see Song of Solomon 5:2,6).

7.
How can we keep out of temptation?

How may we be saved from entering temptation? The answer may be summed up in the words of our Lord, 'Watch and pray'.

1) General directions from 'watch and pray'

a) Make an effort to understand and feel how dangerous it is to enter into temptation

It is frightening to think how careless most people are about the danger of entering into temptation. For most people it is enough that they keep themselves from open sin. To stay out of temptation's reach seems of little importance to them.

In many places (e.g. Proverbs 2:12-20; 4:14-19; 22:24,25; 1 Corinthians 15:33) the Bible warns against the danger of evil company. Yet how many listen to this warning? How many — particularly the young — choose evil friends? It is not long before they are choosing the evil of these friends. In vain many a parent or concerned friend will warn against such companions. At first the young may genuinely dislike some of the things their evil friends enjoy, but, sadly, it is not long before they also enjoy them.

Even more sad is the foolishness of professing Christians who play with temptations they need never have to face. Often, in our day, the Bible's teaching on Christian liberty is abused. Christians feel free to do almost anything they want.

These people claim to be able to hear anything and everything. They claim their Christian liberty. They read what they want and do not listen if wiser Christians condemn what they are reading as false teaching. They will listen to any false teacher. They feel quite confident that they will discern and not be influenced by what they read or hear. What is generally the result of such foolishness? Few, very few, come off without a wound. Many have their faith or sound doctrine overthrown. Nobody has any right to claim a fear of sin who does not fear temptation to it! Sin and temptation are put together by Satan and it is extremely hard for any man to separate them.

In maintaining the principle of Christian liberty we must never forget the equally important principle, 'everything is permissible — but not everything is beneficial' (1 Corinthians 10:23). Do certain places I go to, certain company I keep, certain aims I have, make me cold and careless? Do they hinder my constant and total obedience to Christ? If so, I need to exercise my liberty in avoiding these things. Do I want to avoid entering into temptation? Then I need to be sensitive to my own weakness and depravity. I also need to be aware of the cunning of Satan, the evil of sin and the power of temptation.

We should spend time every day considering the great danger that is involved when we enter temptation. Think of the probable consequences! What an awful thing it is to grieve the Spirit of God, to lose our peace and to put the eternal welfare of our soul in danger. Be sure of this, **if you despise temptation, it will conquer you.** If I am sensitive and watchful here, half the work of avoiding entrance into temptation is done.

b) Be convinced of our inability to keep ourselves from entering temptation

The more clearly we recognise that it is not in our own power to keep ourselves from temptation, the more we will feel our need to pray for help. This is another means of preservation. Most people recognise their need for help once they enter into temptation. At such a time few will trust their own strength to overcome temptation. Rather they will cry out to the Lord for help. The Lord teaches that it is just as important to pray against entering into temptation as to pray for help once we have entered temptation.

Our Lord teaches our need to be kept by the power of God from entering into temptation in two ways. First of all, he teaches us to pray, 'lead us not into temptation' (Matthew 6:13a), and tells us, 'watch and pray so that you will not fall into temptation' (Matthew 26:41a). By teaching us to pray in this way he is showing us that we must place our confidence in God's power and wisdom, not our own, to keep us from temptation. The second way he teaches us is by his own example. He himself prays for his people that they be kept from the evil one (John 17:15). He knows that there are many different ways of entering into temptation. He knows that we can enter into temptation unawares. He knows how powerful temptation is, how deceitful and subtle it can be. He knows our folly, weakness and unwatchfulness. So he has directed us to place our confidence in a higher wisdom and power than we possess in order that we might be kept from entering temptation.

We must learn to speak frequently to ourselves and remind ourselves of such things as these: 'I am poor and weak, Satan is subtle, powerful, cunning and constantly watching for a suitable opportunity to tempt me. The world, especially when it is used as Satan's tool, is attractive, persistent and full of deceitful ways of tempting me. My own sinful nature is strong and always ready to betray me in time of temptation. All about me is an enticing variety of suitable opportunities to satisfy my sinful desires. I am slow to see what is happening. If left to myself I could be ensnared before I knew it. God alone can keep me from falling (Jude 24). I must confidently pray to him alone to keep me from entering into temptation'.

If we faithfully do this, we will find ourselves constantly committing ourselves to the care of God. We shall do nothing and undertake nothing without seeking his will in the matter. Such prayerfulness gives us a double advantage.

i) If we pray in this way we will receive the grace and compassion of God, who has promised to help the weak. We can be sure that those who pray in this way, out of a real sense of need, will never be put to shame.

ii) Maintaining a prayerful spirit of this kind is part of the means God uses to preserve us. If we are aware of our need and looking to God to supply it, we will be careful to apply ourselves to the means God has appointed for our preservation.

c) Exercise faith in God's promise of preservation

To believe that God will preserve us is a means of preservation. If we trust God's promise and pray for preservation he will either keep us from entering into temptation or he will provide a way of escape (1 Corinthians 10:13). God has promised that he will keep us in all our ways (Psalm 91:11), that he will lead us, guide us (Psalm 32:8) and deliver us from the evil one (Romans 16:20).

We must actively trust God's promises and expect him to be faithful to them.

2) A general direction taken from the duty of prayer

Do you wish to be kept from temptation or kept from falling

when tempted? Then you must be much in prayer. Believing that God can preserve us is not enough. God means us to pray for that preservation and God means us to continue in prayer, 'praying always' (Ephesians 6:18, N.K.J.V; cf. Luke 18:1-8). If we do not maintain a constant spirit of prayerfulness, we can expect to be disturbed by a constant stream of temptations.

Every day we should specifically pray for preservation from temptation. We must pray that God would preserve our souls, and keep our hearts and our ways so that we are kept from being trapped by temptation. We must pray that God's good and wise providence will order our ways and affairs so that no pressing temptation will attack us. We must pray that God would give us diligence, carefulness, and watchfulness over all our ways. If we learn to pray in this way, with a real conscious sense of needing God's help, we will experience deliverance.

If we refuse to pray, we shall constantly fall into sin.

8.
What are we watching for?

In this chapter we are going to concentrate upon the other part of our Saviour's direction, namely, to 'watch'. In particular we are going to consider some of the times when we are in danger of 'entering into temptation'.

1) Unusual outward prosperity

A time of unusual outward prosperity is usually accompanied by an hour of temptation. Prosperity and temptation go together. In fact, prosperity is itself a temptation, if not many temptations. Unless God gives special supplies of grace, it is a temptation in two ways. It is likely to provide opportunity for the sinful desires of man; and, the devil knows how to use it for his advantage.

In Proverbs 1:32 we read, 'the prosperity, A.V. (complacency, N.I.V.), of fools will destroy them'. Prosperity hardens them in their way. It makes them despise instruction or warning. The thought of the day of reckoning (which ought to influence them to amend their lives) is put far away. Without the special assistance of God's grace, prosperity can have a devastating influence on believers. This is the argument of Agur, who prays against riches, because of the temptation that accompanies them (Proverbs 30:8,9). This is what actually happened to Israel. 'When I fed them, they were satisfied; when they were satisfied, they became proud then they forgot me' (Hosea 13:6). This is the very danger the Lord warned the Israelites to guard against (Deuteronomy 8, especially verses 12-14).

The believer can rejoice in prosperity (Ecclesiastes 7:14), but he must never forget prosperity brings very real dangers that need to be carefully watched and prayed against. Just think for a moment of some of these dangers.

a) In prosperity, our Christian life is in danger of losing its inner reality. This, as we noted in chapter six, can lay the soul open to all kinds of powerful temptations.

b) In prosperity, we are in danger of taking too much satisfaction and delight from the comforts of this life. Such satisfaction and delight has well been described as 'the poison of the soul'.

c) Prosperity may make us hard and insensitive in our Christian life. If we do not guard against this, it will make us an easy target for the deceitfulness of sin and make us likely to fall into Satan's traps.

In such times of prosperity be thankful to God, but beware of the dangers and devote yourself to 'watching and praying'. Failure to do this has been the downfall of many saints. Wisdom demands that we take heed of their sad experiences. Happy is the man who always fears, but especially does so in a time of prosperity.

2) A sleepy spiritual state

As previously noted (chapter six), if you neglect communion with God and become formal in the exercise of Christian duty, danger is near. This is a time when watchfulness is needed.

If you are in such a state, awake and look about. Your enemy is near. You are in danger of falling into a spiritual condition that you may have to regret for the rest of your life. This state is bad enough as it is, but it is a warning that a worse state may develop. In Gethsemane, the disciples were physically and spiritually sleepy. What did Jesus say to them? 'Watch and pray so that you will not fall into temptation'. We know how near one of them was to a bitter hour of temptation. He immediately entered into it because he was not watching as he ought to have done.

The Beloved in Song of Solomon 5:2-8 was sleepy and unwilling to rouse herself and open the door to her lover. By the time she roused herself, her lover had gone. It was only after much sorrow and pain that she found him again. In the same way, believers may be spiritually sleepy and unwilling to rouse themselves to active communion with Christ. They are likely to bring upon themselves heartache and pain. In many such cases the believer never fully recovers the spiritual vitality he once enjoyed.

The evening that 'David got up from his bed' (2 Samuel 11:1ff) was an evening of spiritual slumber for David. He never fully recovered from his resultant fall. This tragic part of David's history is recorded to warn us. It ought to rouse us to prayerful self-examination.

Some questions for self-examination

i) What benefit are you receiving from your reading of the Scriptures? Are you profiting as much as you used to? Outwardly, others may not see any difference, but is your reading leading you to communion with God?

ii) Is your zeal cold? You may still be doing the same works as before, but is your heart warmed by the love of God? Does the doing of the works warm your heart towards God as it did at the beginning (Revelation 2:2-4)?

iii) Are you becoming negligent in the duties of prayer and hearing the Word of God? You may still be observing these duties, but are you observing them with the same life and vigour as previously (see Luke 8:18; Romans 12:12c)?

iv) Are you growing weary of the Christian life? Or, if you are still keeping up the Christian life, what is your motive for doing so? Do you secretly wish it wasn't such a narrow way (2 Corinthians 4:16-18; 5:14,15)?

v) Are your love and delight in the people of God growing faint and cold? Is your love to them changing from a spiritual love to a carnal love? Is it based upon the things you like about them or the benefits of their friendship rather than their likeness to Christ (1 Thessalonians 4:9,10; 1 Peter 1:22; 3:8)?

Do you find cause for concern in your answers to these questions? Then it is time to awake from your slumber before you fall into some temptation that will cripple you spiritually for the rest of your life.

3) Great spiritual enjoyment

Times of great spiritual enjoyment can often be turned into times of dangerous temptation by the malice of Satan and the weakness of our hearts. Paul knew this. No sooner had he received glorious revelation from God that he was buffeted by a messenger of Satan (2 Corinthians 12:1-9). The three disciples on the Mount of Transfiguration knew this. Peter said, 'Lord it is good for us to be here'. Yet in a very short while they came down the mountain and were faced with demon possession and representatives of an 'unbelieving and perverse generation' (Matthew 17:4; cf. 17:14-17). Jesus himself knew this. When he was baptized he heard a voice from heaven saying, 'This is my Son, whom I love; with him I am well pleased'. Immediately we go on to read, 'Then Jesus was led by the Spirit into the desert to be tempted by the devil' (Matthew 3:17; 4:1).

The devil knows that we can be so full of joy that we fail to watch against his approach. He uses this opportunity to his own advantage. If God blesses you with a spiritual joy, you can greatly rejoice. But do not say, 'I shall never be moved', for you do not know how soon God may hide his face from you, or a messenger from Satan be sent to buffet you. In times of spiritual blessing we need to be especially watchful or a blessing may become a curse.

One other important point about spiritual blessings must be made. There are genuine spiritual blessings that are greatly to be desired; but we must never forget that sometimes people can deceive themselves into thinking that they are filled with a sense of the love of God for them when it is just their own imagination. What havoc such a false experience can lead to. If a person boasts of such experiences of the love of God filling his soul, yet lives as a worldly person, he is self-deceived and in danger of even greater deception.

4) Self-confidence

Temptation is usually near at times when someone is full of self-confidence. Peter gives a painful illustration of this when he boasted, 'Even if all fall away on account of you, I never will... Even if I have to die with you, I will never disown you' (Matthew 26:33,35). It was only a very short time after these words that Peter did what he said he would never do — and wept bitterly for it. God used this fall of Peter to teach him (and us) the foolishness of trusting in ourselves.

The world is full of temptations and false teaching. There are some foolish people who seem confident that they would never fall to these even if everyone else did. Do not be like them! The apostle says, 'Be not high minded, but fear: Let him that thinketh he standeth take heed lest he fall' (Romans 11:20; 1 Corinthians 10:12, A.V.). If we are wise we shall have no confidence in ourselves, but put all our confidence in the keeping power of God.

The first thing about watching is to know what we are watching for. We are watching for the dangerous times in which we are most likely to enter into temptation. In this way, being made aware of the dangers we will be better prepared to deal with them.

9.
How can we guard our hearts against temptation?

In this chapter we are going to continue to consider the subject of 'watching'. In particular we are going to consider a very essential part of this duty described in Proverbs as 'guarding the heart' (Proverbs 4:23). The key is knowing what you are meant to be watching for. In the previous chapter we learned our need to watch for special times when we are most likely to enter into temptation. In this chapter we are going to learn what we need to watch out for. Then we can guard our hearts against entering into temptation.

1) Get to know your own heart

Everybody has his own individual blend of personality and temperament. The better we know the strengths and weaknesses of our personality and temperament the better we can guard our hearts. We also need to know our own specific sinful desires; for example covetousness, selfishness, envy, pride, temper, cruelty, sexual perversion and so on. We need to consider the particular sins that we find attractive; that is, the sins we fall into most. We need to know our spiritual weaknesses; for example doubting, timidity, insensitivity, critical spirit, etc.

When the disciples were not welcomed into a Samaritan village, they asked the Lord if they should call fire down from heaven upon the inhabitants. The Lord rebuked them saying, 'You do not know what manner of spirit you are of' (Luke 9:51-56, N.K.J.). If they had known their spirit, they could have guarded against it. David tells us (Psalm 18:23) that he kept himself from his iniquity, that is, the sin to which he was particularly prone.

Some people are naturally gentle and easygoing. In itself that is a noble nature. When grace reigns, this nature is a great blessing. However, it needs to be watched otherwise its strength can become a weakness. Other people are naturally moody, sour and ill-tempered, so that they very easily fall into envy, malice, selfishness, harsh thoughts of others and many other sins. Others are naturally passionate and they also have a list of sins to which their nature makes them especially prone.

If you want to be kept from temptation, take time to study you own nature. Get to know the kind of person you really are and do not try to justify or excuse the evil and weakness you find. The better you know the evil and weakness of your own heart, the better equipped you are to avoid entering into the temptations to which you are particularly prone. Think of your heart as a place where traitors live. These traitors are your sinful desires and weaknesses. Temptation is always waiting to take advantage of them. Be thankful for any friend who is willing to tell you the kind of person you are and the weaknesses of your nature that you need to guard against. This will be painful, but never forget, 'Faithful are the wounds of a friend' (Proverbs 27:6).

2) Guard your weaknesses

Knowing your weaknesses is not enough. You must also know the ways in which temptation would take advantage of these weaknesses. As we noted in chapter six there are particular occasions, company, individuals, employments, places, etc. that make temptation stronger. For example, if a person has a weakness for gossip, there are certain people and places he should try to avoid. If a person finds that pictures or reports in a newspaper stimulate unclean thoughts, he should take care to avoid them.

The examples that could be given are endless, but no two people will have to avoid exactly the same things. This is one reason why we must be careful not to judge other people's liberty. Each person must get to know what will give temptation an advantage over him and do all he can to avoid these things. Many people can walk through a field of cut grass without suffering from hay fever. The person who does suffer from hay fever will be wise to avoid such a field. In the same way each of us need to know his particular 'allergies' that bring temptation and seek to avoid them.

Obviously, it is not possible to avoid every occasion of temptation. If we are wise, we shall plan to avoid all we can. When duty or providence brings us into an occasion of temptation, we must trust God to keep us.

3) Store the heart with provisions against temptation

We must know the 'traitors' that lurk in our heart. That is not enough. We must also make an effort to store up good treasures in our heart to draw upon in times of temptation. In the old days, sometimes an enemy would come to a fort or castle with the aim of besieging and capturing it. If the enemy found it was well armed and had plentiful supplies and therefore could hold out against him, he would withdraw without attempting to assault it. In the same way, if Satan, the prince of this world, comes and finds us prepared and equipped to resist him, he not only departs, but as James says, he will flee from us (James 4:7).

The particular provision we especially need to store up in our hearts is an awareness of the love of God in Christ. This is the greatest preservative in the world against the power of temptation. Joseph had this when sorely tempted by Potiphar's wife. This enabled him to cry out, 'how then could I do such a wicked thing and sin against God?' (Genesis 39:9). Joseph had stored such a sense of God's love in his heart that even such a pressing and alluring temptation to sin could not hold him. The Apostle Paul says that the love of Christ compels us to live for him (2 Corinthians 5:14). It also constrains us to withstand temptation.

We should also store up in our hearts the provision of the law and the fear of death, hell, and punishment, with the terror of the Lord in them. These provisions, however, are more easily conquered. By themselves they will never stand against a vigorous assault of temptation. These provisions are conquered every day. A heart stored with them will struggle for a while against temptation, but will quickly give in. They must be accompanied by the awareness of the love of God.

What do you need to store in your heart in order to overcome temptation? You need an awareness of the love of God in Christ, a knowledge of the eternal purpose of his grace; a delight in the blood of Christ, and in his love in dying for us. Fill your heart with a delight in the privileges gained by the death of Christ — our adoption, justification, and acceptance with God. Fill the heart with thoughts of the beauty of holiness. That is a gift purchased by Christ. It was the great ultimate purpose of his death — that we might 'be holy and blameless in his sight' (Ephesians 1:4). The heart stored with such riches will, in the ordinary course of walking with God, have great peace and security from the disturbance of temptations.

An awareness of the love of God in Christ may be summed up in the expression, 'the peace of God'. This, the apostle tells us, 'will guard your hearts and minds' (Philippians 4:7). The peace of God is God's special provision against the temptation

58

to worry, as the immediate context indicates. It also guards against all kinds of temptation. The Greek word translated 'guard' is a military word that could be translated 'shall keep as in a garrison'. There are two things that can be said about a garrison. Firstly, it is a place exposed to enemies and secondly, it is a place of safety from the enemy. So it is with our souls. They are exposed to temptations and assaulted continually; but if they are kept in the garrison of God's peace, temptation will not enter, and, as a result, we will not enter into temptation.

4) Keep alert at all times

A guard is on the alert for the first signs of enemy movement. In the same way, the Christian must be on the alert for the first signs of the approach of temptation. Too many Christians are unaware of the approach of their enemy until the enemy wounds them. Their Christian friends may see the warning signs while they themselves are completely unaware of what is happening. Such Christians may be likened to people asleep in a house on fire, unaware of their danger until a friend awakens them to tell them. The process of entering into temptation is often very difficult to discern. This is because so many of the things involved in the temptation may appear quite innocent in themselves.

An illustration of this may be taken from the temptation to the sin of prayerlessness. We are all tempted to this. Very often, the start of this temptation is simply the opportunity of being of help to someone. Little by little, more and more of these opportunities arise until in the end the person finds himself so busy, he is too busy to pray. Who would have thought that the opportunity of helping others would be the start of a temptation leading to such a great evil as a prayerless soul? Many a fearful temptation has begun its course in a deed of thoughtfulness or kindness. One thing has led to another and before the person knows it he is involved in a temptation that is too great for him.

The devil delights in bringing evil out of good. Therefore the Christian needs wisdom and watchfulness in order to avoid the snares that could lead him into temptation. If ever you suspect that a person, an opportunity, a situation, or anything else, is being used as Satan's means of leading you into temptation, do not go a step further until you are sure that the Lord is guiding your footsteps.

5) Consider where temptation leads

If we want to watch against temptation as we should, we need repeatedly to remind ourselves of our enemy. Especially we need to remind ourselves where temptation will lead. We have two active enemies who are always trying to lead us into temptation. We have an enemy within us, a traitor, our sinful desires. We have an enemy outside us, the devil.

We must look upon our sinful desires as our deadly enemy and we must seek grace to hate that enemy as we should. 'Oh that it were killed and destroyed! Oh that I were delivered out of the power of it'. We should long for that every day. Every day we must remind ourselves that the most cursed, sworn enemy is close at hand. This enemy is a traitor in my heart totally committed to my ruin. What madness therefore, if I throw myself into his arms to be destroyed!

Satan is no friend. No, all his friendship would do is to deceive me as a serpent, or devour me as a lion. Always remember, the temptation of Satan has a deeper purpose than even to make you break the law of God. Satan desires more than to tempt you to sin. His ultimate desire is to ruin your soul. If God will not let him ruin your soul, he will still try to assault you with doubts and fears as to your relationship with Christ. Today Satan could suggest to you, 'You belong to Jesus, so you are perfectly safe even if you do sin'. A few hours later, after you have acted upon his advice, he will be telling you, 'You cannot belong to Jesus because if you did you would not have sinned'. Never forget, he is a deadly enemy.

6) Use the shield of faith against temptation

Meet your temptation with thoughts of faith concerning Christ on the cross. If you want to be preserved from entering into temptation, never think of making a truce with it. It cannot be done! Do not debate about it. Resist it by saying, 'It is Christ who died — that died for sins like these'. This is what is meant by 'taking the shield of faith with which you will be able to quench all the fiery darts of the wicked one' (Ephesians 6:16 N.K.J.V). Faith does this by relying on Christ crucified and remembering his love in willingly being crucified and enduring great agonies for our sin. Whatever your temptation may be, it can be conquered by faith in the cross of Christ.

7) What happens if I have failed?

Perhaps you have been surprised by temptation and become caught up with it unawares (as noted in the fourth point). If this is so, what can you do to save yourself from being completely overwhelmed and overpowered by the temptation?

Firstly:
Do as the Apostle Paul did, plead with God again and again that the Lord would 'take it away' (2 Corinthians 12:8). If you persist in this the Lord will either deliver you or do for you as he did for Paul and give you sufficient grace not to be overcome by the temptation. However pressing the temptation may be, never forget that God is able to make it depart. Therefore, pray against the temptation, until it departs or God has renewed your strength to resist and overcome it.

Secondly:
Flee to Christ. Flee to him by faith remembering especially that he knows all about temptation. Plead with him that you 'may

receive mercy and find grace to help you in your time of need' (Hebrews 4:16). When you are tempted and ready to give up, when you want help and feel that you must have it or die — focus your faith on Christ who was also tempted. Consider the temptations he suffered. Remember that he conquered them all. More than that, remember that it was for us that he allowed himself to be tempted and it was for us that he conquered temptation. As you plead, be sure that he will sympathise and come to your help. Lie down at his feet, make your situation known to him, let him know all, beg his assistance and it will not be in vain.

Thirdly:
Look confidently to him who has promised deliverance. Think about the faithfulness of God. This God has promised 'he will not let you be tempted beyond what you can bear' (1 Corinthians 10:13). God cannot fail us! Remind yourself of all God's promises to give us help and deliverance and consider them. Be sure that God has innumerable ways, including many which we do not know about, of giving you deliverance. The following are just a few of the means that he can employ:

a) He can send an affliction that will deaden the particular sinful desire that temptation is offering to satisfy.

b) He can, by some providence, alter the whole situation from which your temptation comes. He can remove the major source of temptation , just like taking away the fuel from a fire. The fire dies out because it has nothing on which to feed itself.

c) He can tread down Satan under your feet, so that, for a time, Satan is completely vanquished. The God of peace will do it (Romans 16:20).

d) He can give you such supplies of grace that you are preserved from being defeated by the temptation even though you are not delivered from the temptation itself.

e) He can give you such comfort in the assurance that good

will come from the temptation that you will feel refreshed in the midst of the temptation and not be harassed by it. This is how Paul could say, 'I delight in weakness, in insults, in hardships, in persecutions, in difficulties, (all powerful forms of temptation) for when I am weak, then I am strong' (2 Corinthians 12:10).

f) He can utterly remove it and make you a complete conqueror.

Fourthly and finally:

Do not forget to find out how you were surprised by this temptation. Look for the way in which this temptation got hold of you. Think of your soul as a boat with a leak that will make the boat sink unless it is plugged. Find the leak and plug it! Find out how temptation managed to get into your soul. Be wise! Ask yourself, when, how, by what means you fell into this trouble. You will probably find that you were negligent or careless, less watchful than usual. If so, plug up the gap by confessing and mourning your failure before the Lord. Trust him to forgive and restore you.

10.
What happens if you do not 'watch and pray'?

Please use your imagination to picture four scenes.

a) Scene One:

Imagine you have been asked to make a hospital visit. The visit has been specially prepared so that you only visit those who are on their deathbeds. Some of the unfortunate people are so thin you can almost count their bones. They have no colour to their skin; they have hardly any strength left and they can barely talk in a whisper. Others are obviously in great pain even though they have been well dosed with pain-killers. Still others are suffering from a variety of very unpleasant diseases. As you go from bed to bed, you ask each patient how they came into their present condition. In every case, the patient tells you what was the start of their condition or how they got the wounds that are slowly killing them. Surely a visit like this would have the effect of making you very careful to try to avoid the things that brought these people to their deathbeds.

b) Scene Two:

Imagine a visit to a country where the death penalty is still carried out. During your visit, you are taken round a prison where you meet all the criminals condemned to death. On meeting each of these criminals you ask the same question: what brought you to this tragic end? Imagine that each prisoner tells you exactly the same story. A visit like this would have the effect of making you take care to avoid the same thing happening to you.

c) Scene Three:

Try to imagine a gathering of Christians who all share one thing in common; they have all entered into temptation and they have all come out of it very badly. All about you are poor, miserable, spiritually wounded souls! — One is wounded by one sin, another by another; one falling into filthiness of the flesh, another of the spirit. Once again, it is your duty to ask all these people how they came into their present condition. With one voice they all agree, 'Alas, we entered into temptation, we fell into cursed snares of the devil and this is the end result'!

d) Scene Four:

Imagine, if it were possible, to visit the realms of the damned in hell and see the poor souls that lie bound in chains of darkness and hear their cries. Listen to what these poor souls say. What are they saying? Are they not cursing their tempters and the temptations they entered into which brought them to this cursed place? The reality of such suffering and anguish defies imagination but that does not alter its reality. Can you think of such things and not take more seriously the danger of entering temptation?

Solomon tells us of the simple ones who follow the adulteress: 'little do they know that the dead are there' (Proverbs 9:18), 'Her house is a highway to the grave' (Proverbs 7:27), and 'her steps lead straight to the grave (Proverbs 5:5). This is the reason that they are so easily enticed and seduced (Proverbs 7:21, 22). It is the same with all kinds of temptation. How few people know that temptation leads to death. Perhaps if people believed this and seriously considered where temptation leads they would be more watchful and careful. Alas, too many people refuse to believe this. They think that they can play with temptation and all will be well in the end. These people forget or ignore the warning, 'Can a man scoop fire into his lap without his clothes being burned? Can a man walk on hot coals without his feet being scorched'? (Proverbs 6:27,28). The answer is a resounding 'NO'! People do not come out of temptation without wounds, burnings and scars.

This world is full of temptation. It is also full of the tragic sight of many who have been tempted to their ruin. It is, therefore, the path of wisdom to heed the Saviour's call to watch and pray. This call is vital. Consider these final thoughts. Perhaps you too can be persuaded to watch and pray.

1) Jesus says, 'watch and pray'

Acting upon this call of Jesus is the only way that God has given to preserve you from entering temptation and falling into sin. Neglect this means and you certainly will fall. Do not flatter yourself that this could not happen to you. Maybe you are a long-established disciple with a holy hatred of sin and think it is impossible that you would ever be seduced into a certain sin. Nevertheless, never forget, 'if you (whoever you may be) think you are standing firm, be careful that you do not fall'.

You may have received much grace in the past; you may have enjoyed wonderful experiences; you may have made great resolve to stand firm. None of these will preserve you from falling unless you prayerfully watch. 'What I say to you', says Christ, 'I say to everyone: **'Watch'!** (Mark 13:37).

Perhaps, in spite of your carelessness in the past, the Lord has preserved you from entering into temptation. If this is so, do not presume on the Lord's continued goodness. Wake up, be thankful for his tenderness and patience, and start watching before it is too late. If you will not perform this duty, you will be tempted in one way or another, to spiritual or fleshly wickedness. You will be defiled. Who knows what the consequences will be? Remember Peter! Remember Judas!

2) Jesus Christ is always watching you

What do you think the Lord Jesus thinks and feels when he sees a temptation hastening towards you and you are fast asleep? It must grieve him to see you exposing yourself to such serious danger after he has given you warning upon warning. When Jesus lived on earth he considered his temptation while it was still on the way. He could say 'the prince of this world is coming. He has no hold on me' (John 14:30b). Dare we be negligent, having his example and knowing that he is watching us? Just try to imagine Christ coming to you as he did to Peter when he was asleep in the garden, with the same reproof; 'are you asleep? Could you not keep watch for one hour? (Mark 14:37). Would you not be grieved if Christ had to reprove you like that? How would you feel to hear Christ thundering against your negligence from heaven, as he thundered against the church of Sardis? (Revelation 3:2).

3) God disciplines those who refuse to watch and pray

If you neglect to watch and pray, the consequences may be twofold. You will certainly fall into sin, sooner or later; also God will be displeased with you and may discipline you. Falling into sin is bad, but God may add to that some discipline or judgement. He will convince you of his anger and displeasure. Remember David, who cried to God after his fall, 'let the bones you have crushed rejoice' (Psalm 51:8). David knew what it was to feel God's chastisement (Psalm 32:4). David's 'pleasure of sin' was very short-lived. The Lord freely and truly forgave him, but he still severely chastened him (see 2 Samuel 12:7-19). If you follow David's example and neglect being watchful you may also have to experience the bitterness of suffering God's displeasure and chastisement.

A last word:
Do not get mixed up with anything which will lead you into temptation. Avoid all appearance of evil and all ways that lead to evil. Especially, watch carefully anything that in the past has caused you to stumble.

'Do not be like the horse or the mule,
which have no understanding
but must be controlled by bit and bridle
or they will not come to you.

Many are the woes of the wicked,
but the Lord's unfailing love
surrounds the man who trusts in him'.

Psalm 32:9,10.

Part two

Putting Sin to Death

Contents

Chapter   **Page**

---

*Note: The modern phrase 'put to death' in Romans 8:13 is translated in the Authorised Version by the word 'mortify'. As this word 'mortify' and its noun form 'mortification' are still in general use in theological writings we will regularly use these words throughout this book.

1.
God's promise and the believer's duty.

In Romans 8:13 the Apostle Paul confronts his readers with two possible ways of life. The first is this, 'if you live according to the sinful nature, you will die.' The alternative is this, 'if by the Spirit you put to death the misdeeds of the body, you will live.' The purpose of this book is to study the second of these ways of life.

We will begin our study by examining the five words or phrases that make up our text:

Firstly, the text begins with the word **'if'**. Paul uses this 'if' to indicate the connection between putting to death the misdeeds of the body and living. It is like telling a sick man, 'if you take the medicine you will soon feel better'. The sick man is being promised an improvement in his health provided he follows the advice he is given. In the same way the 'if' of our text tells us that God has appointed 'putting to death the misdeeds of the body' as the infallible means of achieving 'life'. There is an unbreakable connection between truly putting sin to death and eternal life. 'If...you put sin to death you will live!' Here is the motive for following the duty Paul prescribes.

Secondly, the word. **'you'** tells us to whom the duty and promise apply. 'You' refers to the believers described in v.1 as 'those who are in Christ Jesus'. It refers to those who 'are controlled not by the sinful nature but by the Spirit' (v.9). It refers to those in whom the Spirit lives (vv 10, 11). It is foolish and ignorant to expect anyone other than a true believer to perform this duty. If we think carefully about who Paul is writing to and what he is telling them to do, we can make the following statement:

True believers, who are definitely free from the condemning power of sin, must still make it their business throughout life to put to death the remaining power of sin in them.

Thirdly, the phrase, **'by the Spirit'** refers to the major cause or means of performing the duty. The Spirit here is the same as in v.11. He lives in us (v.9) and gives us life (v.11). He is the Spirit of sonship (v.15) and he helps us in our weakness (v.26). All other ways of trying to put sin to death are useless. People may attempt this work by other means (cf. Romans 9:30-32). They always have and they always will. 'But' says Paul, 'this is the Spirit's work.' Only he can do it. Putting sin to death in your own strength, according to your own ideas, leads to self-righteousness. This is the essence of all false religion.

Fourthly, the phrase, **'put to death the misdeeds of the body'** brings us to the actual duty to be done. Let us consider this phrase by asking and answering three questions:

a) What is meant by **'the body'**? It is another expression similar in meaning to 'the sinful nature' that Paul has frequently referred to in this chapter (see vv.3,4,5,8,12 and 13a). Paul is emphasising the difference between the Spirit and the sinful nature. The body is the instrument that indwelling sin uses to express itself. So Paul uses the expression, 'the body', to represent the natural corruption and depravity of man.

b) What is meant by **'the misdeeds'**? This refers to the sinful actions that a sinful nature produces. In Galatians 5:19

where these acts are described, Paul gives us some examples of these 'misdeeds'. Paul's major concern is not the outward 'misdeeds' but their inward causes. It is the unchecked evil desire that produces such misdeeds which needs to be radically dealt with.

c) What is meant by **'put to death'** ('mortify', A.V.)? This is picture language. Imagine killing an animal. To kill an animal is to take away its strength, power and life so that it cannot act and do what it wants. This is the picture here. The sinful nature (or, remaining sin) is compared to a person, the 'old self', with its resources, abilities, wisdom, cunning, strength etc. This, says Paul, must be put to death. It must be killed (mortified), i.e. its strength, power and life must be taken away by the Spirit.

In one sense this is an accomplished event. The old self is said to be 'crucified with Christ' (Romans 6:6). 'We died with Christ' (Romans 6:8). This happened when we were born again (Romans 6:3-8). Nevertheless, every believer still has the remnants of a sinful nature that will constantly seek to express itself. It is the duty of every believer to put to death the remnants of this sinful nature. This must continually be done so that the desires of the sinful nature are not allowed gratification (cf. Galatians 5:16).

Finally, the phrase, **'you shall live'** provides the promise given to encourage believers in their duty. The life promised is the opposite of the death threatened in the previous case, 'if you live according to the sinful nature, you will die (cf. Galatians 6:8). Perhaps Paul has in mind spiritual life in Christ as well as eternal life. All true believers have this life but they may lose the joy, comfort and strength that such life gives. In a different context the Apostle Paul writes, 'Now we really live, since you are standing firm in the Lord: (1 Thessalonians 3:8) i.e. Now, my life will do me good; I shall have joy and comfort in my life.' Similarly, the apostle is saying here, 'You will lead a good, vigorous, comfortable, spiritual life while you are here, and receive eternal life at the end.'

If we take the promise in this way we have a further motive to perform this duty:

The strength, power and enjoyment of our spiritual life depends on putting to death the acts of the sinful nature.

2.
The lifelong duty of every believer

In the previous chapter we introduced this subject by examining the words and phrases of the text, 'if by the Spirit you put to death the misdeeds of the body, you will live (Romans 8:13b). In this chapter we will concentrate on one important statement from page 74:

True believers, who are definitely free from the condemning power of sin, must still make it their business throughout life to put to death the remaining power of sin.

This same truth is repeated in Paul's exhortation, 'Put to death, therefore, whatever belongs to your earthly nature' (Colossians 3:5). Who is Paul addressing? He is addressing those who have been 'raised with Christ' (Colossians 3:1), who 'died' with Christ (Colossians 3:3), and who 'will appear with him in glory' (Colossians 3:4). Reader, do you put sin to death? Your life depends upon this. Do not stop for a day. Kill sin, or it will kill your peace and joy. Paul tells us what his own practice was in 1 Corinthians 9:27, 'I beat my body and make it my slave'. 'I do it', he says, 'daily.' If this was the daily work of Paul (who was honoured in grace, revelations, enjoyments, privileges, comforts etc. more than most), why should we think we will be exempt from the need to do likewise?

1) As long as we live, remaining sin lives in us.

This is not the place to argue against the foolish notion of sinless perfection in this life. We must be like the Apostle Paul who dared not speak as though we ' have already obtained...or have already been made perfect' (Philippians 3:12). We too recognise our need to be renewed in our inward man 'day by day' (2 Corinthians 4:16). We know we have a 'body of death' from which we are not delivered until the death of our bodies (Romans 7:24, cf. Philippians 3:21). So we admit, remaining sin will live in us, to some extent, till the day we die. This being the case we have no option but to make the killing of sin our daily work. If a person is commanded to kill an enemy and he stops striking before the enemy is dead, he has only done half the work. (See 2 Corinthians 7:1, Galatians 6:9 and Hebrews 12:1).

2) Remaining sin in us is constantly active as long as we live, struggling to produce sinful deeds.

When sin leaves us alone, we can leave sin alone. However, in this life, that will never happen. Sin is deceitful and knows how to appear dead when it is still very much alive. Because of this we must at all times vigorously pursue it to death. Sin is always at work. 'The sinful nature desires what is contrary to the Spirit' (Galatians 5:17). Evil desire tempts us and leads us into sin (James 1:14,15). Sometimes it tries to persuade to evil. Sometimes it tries to hinder from what is good. Sometimes it tries to discourage the spirit from communion with God. As Paul tells us, 'The evil I do not want to do - this I keep on doing' (Romans 7:19). He also tells us, 'I know that nothing good lives in me, that is, in my sinful nature' (Romans 7:18). This stopped Paul from doing good: 'what I do is not the good I want to do' (Romans 7:19). In the same way every believer finds there is a battle when he tries to do good. This is why Paul complains about it so much in Romans 7. Every single day the believer finds a conflict with sin. Sin is always active, always planning, always enticing and tempting. Either sin is defeating us or we are defeating it. It will be like this until the day we die. There is no safety against sin except in a constant warfare against it.

3) If sin is left unchecked, if it is not continually put to death, it will bring about life-dominating, scandalous sins which harm our spiritual life.

Sin always aims at the worst. Every time sin rises to tempt or entice us, it would lead us on to do the worst sin of that kind, if left unchecked. For example, every unclean thought or glance would lead to adultery if it could. Sin, like the grave, is never satisfied. A major aspect of the deceitfulness of sin is the way it starts with small demands. The first advances and suggestions of sin are always very modest. If sin succeeds in its first advance it will make more and more demands until at length, 'just a look at a beautiful woman bathing' ends in adultery, evil scheming and murder (see 2 Samuel 11:2-17). As the writer to the Hebrews warns us, don't allow yourself to become 'hardened by sin's deceitfulness' (Hebrews 3:13). If sin succeeds in its first advance it may simply repeat the initial advance until the heart is less sensitive to sin and is prepared to be drawn a step deeper into sin. The heart is being hardened without really being aware of it, so that sin can make greater demands without the conscience being too disturbed. In this way sin will progress by degrees making increasingly evil demands. The only thing that can prevent sin making this progress is continually putting it to death. Even the holiest saints in the world will fall into the worst of sins if they give up this duty.

4) God has given us his Holy Spirit and a new nature so that we have the means with which to oppose sin and evil desires.

The sinful nature is committed to working against the Holy Spirit and the new nature that God has given the believer. The reverse is also true, i.e. 'the Spirit desires what is contrary to the sinful nature' (Galatians 5:17). Our participation in the divine nature (see 2 Peter 1:4,5) is to enable us to 'escape the corruption in the world caused by evil desires'. If we do not use the Spirit's power and our new nature to put sin to death every day, we neglect the perfect remedy that God has given us against our greatest enemy. If we fail to make use of what we have received God will be perfectly just if he refuses to give us more. God's graces, as well as his gifts, are given to us to use, develop and improve (as taught in the parable of the talents, Matthew 25:14-30). If any Christian fails to put sin to death every day, he is sinning against the kindness, goodness, wisdom and grace of God who has given him the means to do it.

5) Neglect of this duty leads to the decay of grace in the soul and the flourishing of the sinful nature.

There is no surer way of causing spiritual decay than the neglect of this duty. The exercise of grace and victory such exercise brings are the two main ways of making grace strong in the heart. When grace is inactive (like inactive muscle) it withers and decays, and sin hardens the heart. Whenever sin gets a considerable victory, it weakens the spiritual life of the soul (see Psalm 31: 10; 51:8) and makes a believer weak, sick, and ready to die (see Psalm 38:3-5). When poor creatures take (in a spiritual sense) blow after blow, wound after wound, defeat after defeat and never rouse themselves to vigorous opposition, what else can they expect but to be hardened by sin's deceitfulness and for their souls to bleed to death? Sad to say, there is no shortage of examples to illustrate the alarming results of such neglect. Many of us well remember Christians who once were humble, who had tender consciences, who mourned over their shortcomings, who were afraid to offend, who were zealous for the Lord, his work, his day and his people, but who are now changed through neglect of this duty.

They are now earthly-minded, carnal, cold, bitter, following the ideas of this world. This brings shame to true religion and brings great temptation to the people who knew them before.

6) Other duties of the Christian faith cannot be accomplished without the performance of this duty.
It is our duty to be 'perfecting holiness' out of reverence for God (2 Corinthians 7:1), to be 'growing in grace' (2 Peter 3:18). However, these duties cannot be done without the daily mortifying of sin. Sin sets its strength against every act of holiness.

Before we progress to the next chapter of this study it will be helpful to do two things:

a) We will summarise the first general point we have been making in this chapter. It is this: although the believer's death to sin (see Romans 6:2) was purchased for him through the death of Christ, it is still the believer's daily duty to mortify sin. Although we received the promise of complete victory (through conviction of sin, humiliation for sin and the implanting of a new life-principle opposed to sin and destructive of it) when we were first converted, sin remains in the believer. Sin is active in all believers, even in the best of believers, as long as they live in this world. Therefore the constant day to day killing of sin is vital throughout their lives.

b) We will notice two evils which face every believer who fails to put sin to death. The first affects the believer; the second, others.

i) **The believer.** The evil of not taking sin seriously. A person can talk about sin and say what an evil thing sin is, yet if that person is not daily mortifying his own sin he is not taking it seriously. The root cause of failure to mortify sin is that sin is going on without the person realising it. Someone who has the idea that God's grace and mercy allow him to ignore everyday sins is very near to changing God's grace into an excuse to continue sin and being hardened by sin's deceitfulness. There is no greater evidence of a false and rotten heart than this. Reader, beware of such rebellion. It can only lead to the weakening of your spiritual strength if not worse: apostasy and hell. The blood of Jesus is to purify us (1 John 1:7; Titus 2:14), not to comfort us in a life of sin! The exaltation of Christ is meant to lead us to repentance (Acts 5:31). And the grace of God 'teaches us to say "No" to ungodliness' (Titus 2:11,12). The Bible speaks of people who abandon the church because they never really belonged to it (1 John 2:19). The way this happens to many of these people is something like this:

They were under conviction for a while which led them to do certain good works and profess faith. They 'escaped the corruption of the world by knowing our Lord and Saviour Jesus Christ' (2 Peter 2:20), but after they knew the gospel they became tired of its duties. Because their hearts had never been really changed they allowed themselves to neglect various aspects of the Bible's teaching about grace. Once this evil had captured their hearts it was only a matter of time before they plunged their way into hell.

ii) **Other people.** A person who fails to mortify sin by himself may be preserved from actual apostasy yet at the same time exercise a twofold influence upon others:

(a) An influence that hardens others. When others can see so little difference between their own lives and the life of a person who fails to mortify sin in his life they see no need to become Christians. They observe such a person's zeal for religion but they also observe his impatience with those he does not agree with. They observe his various inconsistencies. They see his separation from the world but even more they notice his selfishness and lack of effort to help others. They hear his spiritual talk, his claims of communion with God, but these are contradicted by his conformity to the ways of the world. They hear his boast about the forgiveness of sin but they observe his failure to forgive others. Observing the poor quality of life in such a person, they harden their hearts against Christianity, concluding their lives are just as good as that of any Christian.

(b) An influence deceives others. Others may take such a person as their example of a Christian and assume that because they can follow his example, or even improve upon his example, that they must therefore be Christians as well. In this way such people are deceived into thinking they are Christians while they do not have eternal life.

3.
The work of the Spirit in mortification

In this chapter our attention turns to the believer's dependence upon the work of the Holy Spirit in performing the duty of putting sin to death. The basic truth that this chapter seeks to emphasise may be summarised as follows:

Only the Holy Spirit is competent to do this work. All ways and means to accomplish this work can achieve nothing without his help.
The Holy Spirit works in the believer as he pleases, to direct and empower him in this work.

This summary can be helpfully enlarged under two major headings:-

1) It is pointless to look for other remedies.
Many remedies have been suggested, some of them well-known ones, but they heal nobody. The most religious part of Roman Catholicism is concerned with mistaken ways and means of putting sin to death. This concern expresses itself in wearing sackcloth, vows, religious orders, fastings, penances, etc. All these things are supposed to put sin to death, but they do not.

Unfortunately, such ideas about mortification are not confined to the Roman Catholic Church. There are so-called Protestants, who ought to know better and have the advantage of a clearer understanding of the gospel, who act no better than Roman Catholics. These devote themselves to merely keeping God's law in a way that leads only to pride and has no reference to Christ or his Spirit. Such supposed ways and means of putting sin to death show a deep-rooted lack of acquaintance with God's power and the mystery of the gospel.

There are two main reasons why the efforts of Roman Catholics and so-called Protestants fail truly to put to death a single sin:

a) Because many of the ways and means they insist upon were never intended for this purpose by God. There are no ways and means in true religion that can achieve a particular goal unless God has appointed them for that purpose. Concerning sackcloth, vows, penances and other such things, God asks, 'Who has asked this of you?' (Isaiah 1:12), and says, 'They worship me in vain; their teachings are but rules taught by men.' (Mark 7:7).

b) Because they fail to use God-appointed means in a proper way, e.g. prayer, fasting, watching, meditation etc. These have their proper use in this work but only when used in subordination to the Spirit and faith. Whenever people hope to be successful in killing sin merely by virtue of prayer or fasting so much, they are failing to use God-appointed means in a proper way. As Paul said of some people, in a rather different context, they are 'always learning but never able to come to a knowledge of the truth.' (2 Timothy 3:7, A.V.). Likewise, such people are always trying to put sin to death but never truly doing so. In a word, they have various means to kill the natural man as regards the natural life but none to put to death evil desires which harm the spiritual life.

This is a general mistake made by people who are ignorant of the gospel. It is the cause of much of the superstition and do-it-yourself religion that has come into the world. What injury people have done to themselves, what suffering they have endured, thinking they could slay sin by attacking the physical body instead of the corrupt old self! Self-inflicted whipping or other kinds of torturing of the body (unfortunately, a practice that still persists with some religious people) do nothing to put sin to death.

A more subtle and popular form of this mistake also accomplishes nothing in putting sin to death. It is this: a man is racked with the guilt of a sin which has defeated him. He immediately promises himself and God that he will never do it again. He watches himself, he prays for a while, until his sense of guilty sin regains its former grip. If we consider the true nature of the work that needs to be done in putting sin to death it will be obvious that no amount of self-effort can achieve it. This leads us to our second major heading:

2) Putting sin to death is the work of the Holy Spirit.

Why do we say this? For two reasons:

a) God has promised in his Word to give the Holy Spirit to do this work. The removal of the heart of stone (i.e. the rebellious, stubborn, unbelieving heart) is, in general, this work of putting sin to death that we are considering. It is promised that this will be done by the Spirit, 'I will remove from you your heart of stone ... I will put my Spirit in you' (Ezekiel 36:26, 27).

b) All mortification of sin comes as a gift from Christ and all the gifts of Christ come to us by the Spirit of Christ. Without Christ we can do nothing (John 15:5). Christ gives us our mortification of sin. He is exalted and made Prince and a Saviour, to give repentance to us (Acts 5:31) and our mortification is no small part of that repentance. How does Christ do this? Having received the promised Holy Spirit, he pours him forth for this purpose (Acts 2:33).

In preparation for what will follow in the remaining chapters we will conclude this chapter by considering two important questions:

Firstly, How does the Spirit mortify sin? In general, the Holy Spirit accomplishes this in three ways:

a) He causes our hearts to overflow with grace and produces fruit that opposes the sinful nature at both its roots and its branches. In Galatians 5:19-23 Paul contrasts 'the acts (fruit) of the sinful nature' with 'the fruit of the Spirit'. If the fruit of the Spirit flourishes in a person the sinful nature cannot flourish at the same time. Why is this? Paul answers, 'They (i.e. the sinful nature and the fruit of the Spirit) are in conflict with each other' (Galatians 5:17) and so the two cannot be in the same person in any marked degree. This renewal by the Holy Spirit, as it is called in Titus 3:5, is one major way of putting sin to death. The Spirit causes us to thrive and abound in graces which are opposed to and destructive of the works of the sinful nature and remaining sin itself.

b) He has a dramatic effect on the root and habit of sin - weakening, destroying and removing it. For this reason he is called the Spirit of judgement and the Spirit of fire (Isaiah 4:4). He really destroys and consumes our sinful desires. He begins by removing the heart of stone by an almighty power. He continues as the fire that burns up the roots of evil desire.

c) He brings the cross of Christ into the sinner's heart by faith and gives us communion with Christ in his death and his sufferings. We will turn to this truth again later on.

Secondly, If this is the work of the Spirit alone, why is it a duty that believers are exhorted to perform?

There are at least two answers to this question:

a) Mortification is no more the exclusive work of the Spirit than all other graces and good works are. The Spirit is the author of every grace and good work, yet it is the believer who exercises these graces and actually performs the good works. He 'works in (us) to will and to act according to his good purpose' (Philippians 2:13). 'All that we have accomplished you have done for us' (Isaiah 26:12). See also 2 Thessalonians 1:11; Colossians 2:12; Romans 8:12-13; Zechariah 12:10.

b) The Holy Spirit does not put sin to death in the believer without the believer's obedience and co-operation. He works in us and on us as appropriate to a human nature. He preserves us, our freedom and free obedience. He works in us and with us, not against us or without us. His assistance is an encouragement to do the work and not a reason for neglecting it. The point we are stressing here is simply that this work cannot be done without the Holy Spirit's powerful help. The tragedy is that there are people who are strangers to the Spirit of God, who really do try to put sin to death in their lives and fail. They fight without victory, war with no hope of peace and remain in slavery all their lives.

4.
The value of mortification

In this chapter the truth to be highlighted is that the vitality, strength and comfort of our spiritual life depends a great deal upon our putting sin to death. This truth may best be introduced by explaining two things that it does not mean:

a) It does not mean that provided believers consistently put sin to death they will *automatically* enjoy a vigorous and comfortable spiritual life.
For example, Heman, the writer of Psalm 88, lived a life of constant mortification. Heman was a man who truly walked with God and yet he never enjoyed a good day of peace and consolation. If Heman, such an eminent servant of God, failed to enjoy the peace and consolation that a life of consistent mortification normally brings, we must see that God has a reason for this. God has given Heman as an example to comfort others in a similar condition. While every Christian should use this means of mortification to obtain peace, they should also realise that only God can speak peace and consolation (see Isaiah 57:18,19).

b) It does not mean that mortification is the *major* source through which God gives us a strong and comfortable spiritual life.

Rather, the major sources that give these things are the privileges of our adoption made known to our souls ('the Spirit bearing witness with our spirits that we are the children of God' Romans 8:16). The Spirit's ministry of assuring us of our adoption and justification is the major source of a vigorous and comfortable spiritual life.

Let us turn now and see what this truth does mean:
In our normal relationship with God and in his normal dealings with us, a strong and comfortable spiritual life depends to a great extent on our consistent mortification of sin. As a *general* rule, mortification has an effectual influence in the production of a strong and comfortable spiritual life. Three considerations will help to prove this point:

1) Nothing but the mortification of sin will keep it from depriving a spiritual life of its vigour and comfort.
Every sin that isn't put to death will certainly accomplish two things:

a) It weakens the soul and deprives it of its strength. When David permitted an unmortified sinful desire to linger in his heart it left him with no spiritual strength. 'There is', said David, 'no health in my body; my bones have no soundness because of my sin...I am feeble and utterly crushed' (Psalm 38:3,8). An unmortified sinful desire will dry up the spirit and all the strength of the soul and thus weaken it for all duties. It does this in three ways:

First - it unsettles the spiritual well-being of the whole heart. It does this by diverting the heart from the spiritual state that is necessary for vigorous communion with God. This diversion is gained by capturing the desires of the heart with worldly desires so that the love of the Father is expelled.

90

Second - it works on the mind, prompting thoughts intended to encourage the gratification of sinful desires. It will aim to exaggerate the pleasures of sin and supply reasons why sinful desires should be gratified.

Third - It breaks out and actually hinders duty. It does this by appealing to a man's particular sinful desires. For example, when an ambitious man ought to be engaged in the worship of God it will drive him to substitute study for worship of God.

b) As sin weakens, so it also darkens, the soul and deprives it of its comfort and peace. Sin is like a thick cloud that spreads itself over the face of the soul and cuts off all the beams of God's love and favour. It takes away a person's awareness and enjoyment of the privilege of his adoption.

Mortification is the only remedy against these two evil effects of sin upon the soul.

2) Mortification also has a very beneficial effect upon the growth of God's graces in the human heart.

If the human heart is likened to a garden then mortification may be likened to the work of removing the weeds that would hinder the growth of God's plants of grace. Think of a garden where a precious herb has been planted. If the garden is regularly weeded the herb will flourish. If, however, weeds are left the herb will be a poor, withering and useless plant. Where mortification fails to destroy the weeds of sin, the plants of God's grace are ready to die (Revelation 3:2). They are withering and decaying. Such a heart is like the sluggard's field — so overgrown with weeds that you can hardly see the good corn. When you look in such a heart, the graces of faith, love and zeal are there; yet they are so weak, so clogged with the weeds of sin, that they are of very little use. Let such a heart be weeded of sin by mortification and these plants of faith, love and zeal will begin to flourish and be ready for every good use and purpose.

3) Mortification is a means through which God can give peace to the soul.
Sincerity is a major foundation upon which true peace of soul rests. Mortification is one of the clearest evidences of a person's sincerity. Let a man evidence his sincerity by the vigorous opposition of his soul to self and that man should enjoy a safe sense of peace in his soul.

5.
An introduction to the practice of mortification

In this chapter we shall start dealing with some of the questions and practical difficulties that believers are involved in when they work at their duty of mortification. We can best introduce this subject with a description of the kind of problem that believers generally have to struggle with. It is this:

We have a true believer who finds in himself a powerful indwelling sin that repeatedly brings him into bondage, eats up his heart with trouble, hinders him in his communion with God and generally disturbs his peace. This indwelling sin troubles his conscience and even exposes the believer to being hardened through the deceitfulness of sin. The question is, what is the believer to do about this? What course shall he take to deal with this sinful desire that repeatedly hinders his spiritual life and growth? How can the believer mortify this sinful desire to such a degree that, though it is not utterly destroyed, yet he is generally able to triumph over it and enjoy peace in his communion with God? In answer to this question we will aim to do three things:

1. Explain what is involved in the putting to death (mortification) of any sin. As this is so basic to our understanding of the whole subject we must show what it does not mean as well as showing what it does mean.

2. Give general directions that are essential to the true and spiritual mortification of any sin.

3. Give specific directions as to how this can be done.

1) A negative and positive explanation.

a) In the remainder of this chapter we will explain five things that mortification does not mean and in the next chapter we will explain three things that mortification does mean.

i) **To mortify a sin is not to destroy it utterly and eradicate it from the heart.** It is true to say that this is the aim of mortification, but it is an aim that will not be accomplished in this life. Doubtless, the believer can expect wonderful triumphs over sin by the help of the Spirit and the grace of Christ, so much so that he may have almost constant victory over sin. But he is not to expect the total destruction and eradication of sin in this life. Paul assures us of this in Philippians 3. Paul knew that in spite of all his attainments he was not yet perfect (v.12). This knowledge didn't hinder a 'lowly body' (i.e. a body that still has indwelling sin) from being changed by the transforming power of Christ at his return (v.21). God sees it best that in ourselves we should be complete in nothing, that in all things we must be complete in Christ (Colossians 2:10).

ii) **To mortify sin (and this hardly needs to be said!) is not to try to disguise it.** Sad to say, a person can outwardly forsake the practice of many sins while still having the desire to do them. People may think of that person as a changed man. But such a person has only added to former sins the cursed sin of hypocrisy and so found a more sure path to hell.

iii) **To mortify sin does not necessarily mean the cultivation of a quiet, sedate nature.** Many people are naturally blessed with a pleasant temperament. They are easygoing and not inclined to lose their temper. Now, such people can cultivate and improve their pleasant nature by discipline, consideration and prudence and appear to themselves and others as very spiritual. The tragedy is that one person is hardly ever troubled with anger or passion whilst another person has to contend with these sins every day; and yet it is possible that the second person has done more to put sin to death than the first person. Let the first person judge himself by his selfishness, unbelief, envy, or some such spiritual sin. This will give him better idea of his true state before God.

iv) **A sin is not mortified when it is only diverted into another direction.** Simon (see Acts 8:9-24) left his practice of sorcery for a while; but the covetousness and ambition which lay behind his sorcery remained and acted in another way. In spite of all Simon's apparent new way of life (v.13) he was still 'full of bitterness and captive to sin' (v.23). Whoever substitutes pride for worldliness, or legalism for sensuality, need not think that the sin that seems to have been left behind has been mortified!

v) **The occasional conquest of sin doesn't amount to mortification.** Let us look at two examples of this:

a) A sin breaks out and brings terror to the conscience and dread of scandal as well as fear of God's displeasure. This can have the effect of waking a person from spiritual slumber and for a while they are filled with abhorrence of that sin and put on guard against it. However, the sin remains unmortified. The sin is like an enemy who has crept into the camp and murdered one of the captains. Immediately, the guards are on the alert and searching through the camp to find the enemy. The enemy hides himself while the guards search through the camp. For a while it might seem that the enemy is vanquished; but he is unharmed and waiting for another opportunity to do the same thing again.

b) In a time of some judgement, calamity or pressing affliction, the heart is concerned about how to be relieved of these things. A person may believe that such relief can only be gained by dealing with his sin, so that he resolves to forsake it. However, sin is so deceitful and it is content to lie quiet for a while and give the appearance of being put to death. It is far from mortified and sooner or later it will spring to life again. In Psalm 78:32-37 there is an excellent illustration of all this. When trouble came these people were quick to turn to the Lord. This they did 'eagerly' with earnestness and diligence; but yet their sin was unmortified (vv.34, 37).

By these and many other ways poor souls can deceive themselves and think they have mortified their evil desires when really the sins still live and are waiting for suitable occasions to break out and disturb their peace.

6.
A positive explanation of mortification

Now we turn to an explanation of what mortification is. There are three things that mortification accomplishes:

1) An habitual weakening of evil desire.
Every lust (evil desire) is a depraved habit that continually inclines the heart to evil. In Genesis 6:5 we have a description of an unmortified heart, 'Every inclination of the thoughts of his heart was only evil all the time.' In every unconverted man there is an unmortified heart that is full of a variety of ungodly desires and each of these desires is continually crying out for satisfaction.

We will just concentrate upon the mortification of one such evil desire. This desire (think about the sin most applicable to you) is a strong, deeply-rooted, habitual inclination and bias of the will and of the feelings to a particular actual sin. One of the great evidences of such an evil desire is the tendency to think about ways in which this particular evil desire can be gratified (see Romans 13:14). This sinful habit (i.e. lust or evil desire) works violently. It 'wars against the soul' (1 Peter 2:11) and seeks to make a person 'a prisoner of the law of sin' (Romans 7:23). Now the first thing that mortification accomplishes is the weakening of this evil desire so that it becomes less and less violent in its efforts to provoke and entice to sin (see James 1:14,15).

At this point a warning needs to be given. All evil desires have the power to entice and provoke to sin, but they don't all appear to have the same power. There are at least two reasons why some evil desires appear much more powerful than others:

i) One evil desire may be stronger than others in the same person and also stronger than the desire in another person. There are many ways in which this extra life and power is given but especially through temptation.

ii) The violent actings of some evil desires are far more obvious than others. Paul puts a difference between uncleanness and all other sins. 'Flee from sexual immorality. All other sins a man commits are outside his body, but he who sins sexually sins against his own body' (1 Corinthians 6:18). This means that sins of this kind are more easily discernible than others. Nevertheless, a man with an inordinate love of the world may be just as much under the power of that evil desire (though its power is not as obvious) as another man who is captivated by an evil desire or sexual immorality.

The first thing, then, that mortification accomplishes is the gradual weakening of the violent actings of evil desire so that its power to impel, stir up, trouble and perplex the soul is diminished. This is called crucifying 'the sinful nature with its passions and desires' (Galatians 5:24). This language is very graphic, as can be seen from the following illustration:

Think of a man nailed to a cross. At first the man will struggle and strive, and cry out with great strength and might. After a while, as his blood drains away, his strivings grow faint and his cry becomes low and hoarse. In the same way when a man first sets about the duty of putting an evil desire to death there is a violent struggle; but as the 'blood and spirits' of the evil desire drain away its 'strivings and cries' diminish. Now the initial, radical mortification of sin is described in Romans 6 and especially in verse 6:

'For we know that our old self was crucified with him'—
For what purpose?—'so that the body of sin might be
rendered powerless, that we should no longer be slaves
to sin.'

Without this initial, radical mortification accomplished through union with Jesus Christ, as described in Romans 6 (more will be said about this in the next chapter), a person cannot make any progress in mortifying a single evil desire. A man can beat down the bitter fruit from an evil tree until he is weary. But as long as the root remains in strength and vigour no amount of beating down the fruit will hinder the root from bringing forth more evil fruit. This is the foolishness that many people display when they set themselves with all earnestness against the breaking out of particular sins but never actually attack and wound the root of sin itself (as is done when a believer is united to Jesus Christ).

2) A constant fighting and contending against sin.
When sin is strong and vigorous the soul can make little spiritual progress. Unless we constantly fight against sin, it will grow strong and vigorous and spiritual progress will be constantly hindered. There are three major things involved in contending with sin. They are:

a) We must know our enemy and be determined to destroy our enemy by all means possible. We have to remind ourselves that we are in a conflict that is vigorous and hazardous, a conflict that has serious consequences. We need to be 'aware of the afflictions ('plague', A.V.) of our own heart' (1 Kings 8:38). We must guard against thinking lightly of this plague. It is to be feared that too many have little knowledge of the great enemy they carry with them in their hearts. This makes them ready to justify themselves and to be impatient of reproof or admonition, not realising they are in any danger (see 2 Chronicles 16:10).

b) We must work to know the ways of our enemy, the strategies and methods of warfare employed, the advantages our enemy seeks to take and even occasions when the enemy attack is most successful. The better we know these things the better we will be prepared to fight and contend with sin. For example, if we observe that our enemy repeatedly takes advantage of us in a particular situation then we will seek to avoid that situation. We must seek to set the wisdom of the Spirit against the craftiness of indwelling sin so that we can quickly see through the cunning of our enemy and frustrate his evil plans against us.

c) We must work daily to use every means that God has ordained to wound and destroy our enemy (some of these will be mentioned later). We must not allow ourselves to be lulled into a false sense of security and think that our sinful desires are dead because they are quiet. Rather, we need to give these sinful desires fresh wounds and new blows every day (see Colossians 3:5).

3. Success in our opposition and conflict with indwelling sin.

When there is frequent success against any evil desire this is another part and evidence of mortification. By success we mean a victory over it accompanied with the intention to follow up that victory and strike again. For example, when the heart detects the workings of indwelling sin (trying to seduce, entice, work on the imagination, etc.), it instantly arrests sin, exposes it to the law of God and love of Christ, condemns it and executes it.

When a person knows such success that the root of evil desire is actually weakened, and that its activity is curtailed so that it can no longer hinder his duty or interrupt his peace as it used to, then sin has been mortified in some considerable measure.

This weakening of the root of evil desire is mainly accomplished by the implanting, habitual residence, and cherishing of the spiritual life of grace that stands in direct opposition to evil desire and is destructive of it (cf. chapter 4, p. 91, point 2). So, by the implanting and growth of humility, pride will be weakened. In the same way patience will deal with passion; purity of mind and conscience will deal with uncleanness; heavenly-mindedness will deal with love of this world and so on.

7.
General rules for the practice of mortification

There are some general rules and principles that are essential to evangelical mortification. Without these no sin will ever be mortified. In this chapter we will look at the first and most basic of these rules. It is this:

Only a believer, i.e. a person who is truly united to Christ, is capable of mortifying a single sin.

As we noted in the very first chapter (see p. 74 paragraph 4), mortification is the work of believers: 'If...**you** put to death...' (Romans 8:13). An unregenerate man (i.e. a person who is not truly united to Christ by faith) may do something like mortification but he cannot mortify a single sin in a manner acceptable to God. In chapter 3 we noted how many sincerely religious people (acting upon the principles taught to them by their church) attempt to mortify their sin but, alas, all in vain.

We are not suggesting that only believers are obliged to mortify sin. No, mortification is a duty (like repentance and faith) that God requires of all who hear the gospel. What we are insisting on is that only the believer can do this. The unbeliever is also obliged to do this but it is not his immediate duty. His immediate duty is to believe the gospel that he has heard.

Without the aid of God's Spirit mortification cannot be done. A man may more easily see without eyes, or speak without a tongue, than truly mortify one sin without the Spirit. But how can a person gain the help of God's Spirit? He is the Spirit of *Christ* and he is received by believing the good news about Jesus Christ — not as a reward for keeping the law (see Galatians 3:1-5, especially v.1). All attempts to mortify any lust without faith in Jesus Christ will prove worthless.

When the Jews were convicted of their sins on the day of Pentecost and cried out, 'What shall we do?', what was Peter's response? Did he direct them to mortify their pride, anger, malice, cruelty etc.? No; he knew that wasn't what they needed to do then. What they needed was to be converted, to repent of their sins and believe in Jesus Christ (see Acts 2:38). Peter knew that man's first need was to trust in him whom they had pierced' and that if he did this, true humiliation and mortification would result. The same was true of the ministry of John the Baptist. The Pharisees laid on the people heavy duties and rigid means of mortification such as fastings and washings. John, however, preached the immediate necessity of conversion and repentance (see Matthew 3:8).

The ministry of Christ was the same. He said, 'Do people pick grapes from thornbushes?' (Matthew 7:16). Trees can only produce fruit after their kind and so Christ tells us, 'Make a tree good and its fruit will be good' (Matthew 12:33). In other words, the root must be dealt with. The nature of the tree must be changed or it is impossible for the tree to produce good fruit.

This fact is so basic, but so important, that we must spend a little more time considering some of the dangers that arise when it is neglected or ignored. We will just focus on three dangers:

1) The danger of being diverted from man's primary duty.

When this basic fact is ignored or neglected there is the danger that a man's mind and soul become preoccupied with a duty that is not really his proper business. Man's primary business is to repent and believe the gospel. Until this is done no other duty has any real value. A man can spend all his efforts trying to mortify sin when he ought to be spending all his efforts to gain a saving faith in Christ.

2) The danger of self-delusion.
The duty of mortification is a good thing in itself, provided it is only undertaken by those who have a saving faith in Christ. The danger is that a person can apply himself to this duty and assume that because he does this he must be pleasing to God. For example:-

a) Instead of going to the Great Physician of souls for healing through his death on the cross, a man can busy himself trying to heal himself through the duty of mortification. 'When Ephraim saw his sickness, and Judah his sores, then Ephraim turned to Assyria and sent to the great king (Jareb) for help' (Hosea 5:13) and thus Judah and Ephraim were kept from the healing God could have given them.

b) Because the duty of mortification seems to have a great evidence of sincerity about it a man can become hardened by it in a kind of self-righteousness and think that his state is good.

3) The danger of being disillusioned by lack of success.
An unbeliever may sincerely work at this duty yet only deceive himself. Sooner or later he will find that his sin is not being mortified and that he is simply changing one kind of sin for another. He will then despair of ever being successful and give himself up to the power of sin.

Conclusion

Mortification is the work of faith, the special work of faith. Now if there is a work to be done that can only be done in one particular way, it is utter foolishness to attempt to do it in any other way. It is faith that purifies the heart (Acts 15:9); or, as Peter informs us, we purify our 'souls in obeying the truth through the Spirit' (1 Peter 1:22); and without faith, it will not, **cannot**, be done. What we have written in this chapter should be enough to verify the first general rule of mortification: **Be sure that you are united to Christ by faith because, if you intend to mortify any sin without such a union, you will not succeed.**

Postscript: A possible objection and some answers

There is one major objection to this first general rule of mortification which may be put in the form of a question:

What should the unregenerate man who is convicted of the evil of sin be encouraged to do? Is such a person just to cease striving against sin, live dissolutely, give full vent to lusts and be as bad as the worst of men?

The short answer to such a question is simple. God forbid! (John Owen then goes on to give four reasons why it is right to encourage unregenerate men to strive against sin. We will just focus on the first and last of these):

a) Consider the wisdom, goodness and love of God shown in the variety of ways he restrains men and women from being as bad as they could be. Whatever way this is done, it is the outcome of God's care, kindness and goodness, without which the whole earth would be a hell of sin and confusion.

b) Mortification is a duty unregenerate people are responsible to perform, but it is not their first duty. If a man is mending a hole in the wall of his house he won't think I'm his enemy if I come and tell him to leave the hole for a while and put out a fire which threatens to burn up his whole house. If a man has a sore finger and a raging fever it is the raging fever that needs to be dealt with first and then the sore finger can be dealt with.

The same is true in the spiritual realm. It is no use wearying yourself fighting a particular sin when your real problem is a sinful nature that is in bondage to sin. First of all bring your sinful nature to Christ the great Physician, then, when he has delivered you from the bondage of a sinful nature, you are ready to start mortifying particular sins.

8.
The second general rule for mortification

The first rule was concerned with what a person needs to be before he is capable of performing the duty of mortification. The second rule concerns the attitude necessary to perform this duty. The attitude may be summed up in the following rule:-

You will not put to death any sin unless you sincerely and diligently seek to deal with all sin.

To put it very simply, the believer is not given the option of deciding which sin in his life needs to be mortified. Unless the believer is committed to dealing with each and every sin in his life he will never succeed in mortifying a single sin. Let me explain what I mean a little more fully.

A believer is tried by a sinful desire like that described at the beginning of chapter five. This sinful desire (think of what is most applicable to you) troubles the believer. It repeatedly defeats him and plagues him so that he longs for complete deliverance. Not only that, he actually strives against that sin, prays and mourns when he is defeated by it. At the same time, however, there are other duties of the Christian life that he doesn't take very seriously. He can go days without enjoying real communion with God. He can read his Bible in a very casual way, neglecting to meditate upon that word of God and spends little or no time in prayer. These neglected or poorly performed duties of the Christian life are sins (sins of omission), but they don't trouble him like the sin he longs to be delivered from. Now, the point we are seeking to emphasise is that this believer need not expect to get deliverance from the sin that really troubles him until he starts treating the other sins with the same seriousness.

Why is this? There are two reasons:

a) This attempt at partial mortification is based upon a false reasoning. Without hatred of sin as sin (not simply hatred of its disturbing consequences) and a sense of the love of Christ on the cross, there can be no true spiritual mortification. Now this attempt at mortification gives no evidence of being motivated by a hatred of sin as sin and a sense of the love of Christ on the cross. Rather, the motive is simply self-love. A particular sin disturbs this person's peace and wellbeing, so he battles with this sin simply to regain them.

To such a person a faithful pastor would need to say:

> Friend, you have neglected prayer and Bible reading. You have been careless about the example your life gives to others. These are just as much sins and evils as the sin you are trying to conquer. Jesus bled for these sins also. Why haven't you made an effort to conquer them? If you really hated sin as sin you would be just as watchful against everything that grieves and disturbs the Holy Spirit as you are about this particular sin that grieves and disturbs your own soul. Don't you see that your battle with sin is simply concerned with your own peace and wellbeing? Do you think that you can expect the Holy Spirit to help you get rid of the sin that disturbs you when you show no concern to deal with other sins that grieve him just as much?

Whatever we may think, the work of mortification that God requires is a total commitment to the mortification of all sin. If a believer sincerely aims to do what God requires, he can depend on the help of his Spirit. If the believer is only concerned about doing his own work (i.e. simply trying to mortify the sins that trouble him) God will leave him to struggle in his own strength. The command is 'let us purify ourselves from **everything that contaminates** the body and spirit, perfecting holiness out of reverence for God' (2 Corinthians 7:1). If we do anything, we must aim at doing everything.

b) Sometimes God employs a strong unmortified sinful desire in a believer as a means of chastening him. When a believer grows lukewarm (Revelation 3:16ff) and careless in his walk with God, God sometimes permits a sinful desire to grow strong in his heart so that it becomes a plague and a burden to him. This can be one of God's ways of chastening a believer for disobedience, or at least of awakening him to consider his ways and call him to a full-hearted mortification of sin. An example similar to this can be seen in God's dealings with Israel in the days of the Judges (see, for example, Judges 1:27-2:3 - especially 2:3).

Note 1: When a believer is plagued by a particular sinful desire that is so strong that he hardly knows how to control it, this is generally the result of a careless walk with God or an unwillingness to take seriously the warnings of Scripture.

Note 2: Sometimes God uses the plague of a particular sinful desire to prevent or cure some other evil. This was God's purpose in allowing a messenger of Satan to trouble Paul to keep him 'from becoming conceited because of the surpassingly great revelations' he received (see 2 Corinthians 12:7). Likewise, it could well be that Peter was left to deny his Lord as a means of correcting his over-confidence in himself.

Conclusion of this section

Whoever wants to mortify any troublesome lust in his life thoroughly and acceptably, must take care to be equally diligent in obedience to all the duties God calls him to. Also, let him know that every sinful desire, every omission of duty, is burdensome to God. As long as there is a treacherous heart that is prepared to neglect the need to strive for obedience in every area, there is a weak soul that is not allowing faith its whole work. Any soul in such a weak condition has no right to expect success in the work of mortification.

9.
The first particular rule for mortification

In the previous two chapters we considered two general rules essential for the mortification of any sin. In this chapter we begin to consider the more particular rules, or directions, to guide a believer in the duty of mortification. The first of these rules is to prepare the believer for this:

A careful diagnosis of the sinful desire to be mortified

The first thing a good doctor does when someone comes requiring treatment for an illness is to give his patient a careful examination. By doing this the doctor tries to find out all the symptoms connected with the illness. For example, he may take the patient's temperature and check his pulse and blood pressure. He will ask questions about when the illness started. The various things the doctor observes (e.g. a high temperature, a rash or spots, swelling, pain, etc.) and the things he finds out about the illness, will all help the doctor decide the exact illness that needs to be treated. This is known as the diagnosis. A good doctor will never simply prescribe pain killers because the patient is in pain. He wants to know what it is that is causing the pain (i.e. the disease or illness) before he prescribes any medicine.

In the same way we can think of sinful desire as being like a disease that needs to be correctly diagnosed before it can be treated. Some have more worrying symptoms than others. These will not be mortified using the same remedy as used for another sinful desire with less worrying symptoms. This leads us to consider some of the worrying symptoms that will tell us if we need to use a stronger remedy than usual.

1) A firmly established sinful desire.
A sinful desire that has been allowed to corrupt the heart for a long time without any vigorous attempt to mortify it or heal the wounds it has caused is a dangerous one. Such a sinful desire brings the soul into the woeful condition that David describes in Psalm 38:5: 'My wounds fester and are loathsome because of my sinful folly.' In such a case the ordinary course of humiliation will not succeed in mortifying it. It has corrupted the conscience to the extent that the sinful desire and the conscience can live together without taking much notice of each other. The sinful desire does what it wants, more or less, and the conscience hardly knows what is going on. At one time the conscience would have been greatly alarmed at what now goes on in the heart; now it is almost asleep.

Such a sinful desire needs to be treated with the same seriousness that a good doctor will use to treat an old neglected wound. The doctor knows such wounds are always dangerous and often fatal. Maybe the danger of this sinful desire will best be seen by considering the following very solemn question:

How can a person be sure that his firmly established sinful desire isn't simply the dominion of sin and that he has never been truly born again?

A sinful desire that is allowed to continue in ease and quiet is just like rust; it can only be removed with great difficulty. Sinful desire never dies of itself, so if it is not daily subdued it will simply gather strength.

112

2) A heart that wants peace without a fight.

This is another dangerous symptom of the power of sinful desire to corrupt a believer's heart. In this case it has captured the heart to the extent that the heart doesn't want to destroy it but the heart does want to enjoy peace. This symptom may be recognised in a few different ways but we will confine ourselves to two examples:

a) A believer is troubled in his thoughts by a sinful desire. His conscience is disturbed and he feels unhappy. Instead of deciding to mortify this sinful desire the believer searches his heart to find other evidences that he is a Christian. By doing this he hopes that in spite of having a sinful desire that he refuses to mortify, he can have peace of heart because he knows he is a Christian. When a symptom like this can be recognised in a believer, that believer is in a dangerous spiritual condition.

It was a spiritual condition like this that was the ruin of many Jews in the days of Jesus. Under the preaching of Jesus the consciences of many Jews were disturbed but, rather than acknowledge and mortify their sinful desires, they clung to their status as 'Abraham's descendants' and thought they were accepted by God (see John 8:31-41). This is a dangerous symptom of a heart in love with sin, a heart that underestimates the enjoyment of peace with God and every token of God's love. How corrupt a heart has become when it plainly shows that its owner will be well content to remain an unfruitful Christian, as long as he can hope to escape the 'wrath to come'. What a tragedy when a believer can feel content to be at any distance from God, as long as it is not final separation. What can be expected of a heart like this?

b) As in the first example we have a believer who is troubled in his thoughts by a sinful desire. His conscience is disturbed and he feels unhappy. This time, instead of deciding to mortify this sinful desire the believer seeks to remove his distress of soul by pleading the grace and mercy of God. It is as if the believer (like Naaman worshipping in the house of Rimmon - see 2 Kings 5:18) is pleading, 'In every other way I will walk with God, but in this thing, God be merciful to me.' Such behaviour is quite inconsistent with Christian sincerity, and is usually strong evidence that the person behaving like this is a hypocrite. There is little doubt, however, that some of God's children can be trapped by this sinful deceit.

Whenever a believer's heart secretly likes sin so that the believer is prepared to escape the distress of this in some other way than mortification and pardon of sin through the blood of Christ, then that man's 'wounds fester and are loathsome'. Unless there is a speedy remedy, that man is very near to spiritual death.

3) A frequently successful sinful desire.

When a sinful desire frequently succeeds in obtaining the consent of the will to do what it wants, this is another dangerous symptom. This symptom needs some further explanation. When a particular sinful desire gets the consent of the will with some delight, even though an outward act of sin is not committed, the sinful desire has been successful. There are many reasons that can prevent a person from going as far as the outward act of sin; but as long as the person is willing to do the sin, provided nothing prevents him, sinful desire has succeeded in gaining the consent of the will. It is doubtless true that sinful desire has its occasional success in the best of men. However, when it frequently succeeds in this way it is the symptom of a dangerous spiritual condition.

Note: One reason why sinful desire can have this frequent success even in true Christians, is because it manages to take them by surprise. No Christian should think that this lessens the danger of their spiritual condition. The Christian ought not to be taken by surprise because this could be avoided by carrying out his duty to watch and pray.

4) The use of legal motives for fighting against sinful desire.
When the only motive for mortifying sin is a fear of the consequences, that is a very dangerous symptom of an unhealthy spiritual state. There are proper Christian motives for mortifying sin. For example, Joseph reasons, 'How then could I do such a wicked thing and sin against God?' (Genesis 39:9). It was love for a good and gracious God that motivated Joseph. Likewise the Apostle reasons, 'for Christ's love compels us...' (2 Corinthians 5:14). For a man to be motivated to oppose sin simply by the fear of shame among men, or hell from God, is a sure sign of a heart that is far from healthy.

Note:
 i) Paul's main argument to prove that sin shall not be the master of believers is that they 'are not under the law but under grace' (Romans 6:14). If your fight against sin is motivated only by the principles of the law, what assurance can you have that sin shall not have dominion over you and ruin you?

ii) If a person's sinful desire has managed to make him abandon gospel remedies against it, there is no hope that a remedy of the law will succeed.

5) When God uses sinful desire as a chastisement.
Although God sometimes employs a strong unmortified sinful desire in a believer as a means of chastening that believer (as noted in chapter 8), this is also a way that God deals with an unbeliever. Therefore, when a believer has reason to believe that God is chastening him in this way he must judge this symptom as serious and dangerous. He must not rest until he has dealt with the cause of his chastisement.

This raises the question: How can a believer know if a strong unmortified sinful desire in his life is being employed by God to chasen him?

Answer: Examine your heart and your ways. What was the state and condition of your soul before you became entangled with the sinful desire which is now such a trouble to you? Were you neglecting your Christian duties? Were you living with too much concern for your own wellbeing and too little concern for others? Was there the guilt of some great sin that you have never repented of?

Had you received any special mercy, protection or deliverance from which you did not benefit as you could have, nor were thankful for? Had you been exercised by some affliction but never tried to find out God's purpose for it? Had God, in his gracious providence, given you opportunities to glorify him which you failed to take? These are some of the questions you must ask yourself. If you are convicted by any of them, repent and seek the Lord's forgiveness.

6) When a sinful desire has withstood God's special dealings.

An example of this condition is described in Isaiah 57:17:

'I was enraged by his sinful greed; I punished him, and hid my face in anger, yet he kept on in his wilful ways.'

God had dealt with the sinful desire of greed in two different ways but the people were so in love with it that they paid no attention to him. This is a very serious condition. Only the sovereign grace of God (as expressed in the next verse - 'I will heal him...') can deal with such a condition.

In a similar way God deals with the various sinful desires of his people in all ages. God especially does this through his Word by the convicting power of his Spirit (when the Word is read or preached). When a sinful desire has such a control over a man that he can ignore this convicting power and continue to leave sin unmortified, he is in a very dangerous state.

These symptoms, and others not mentioned, are evidences of a sinful desire that is dangerous, if not deadly. Such sinful desires cannot be mortified in the ordinary way. A more powerful remedy is needed.

116

A WORD OF CAUTION

While the worrying symptoms we have just mentioned may be present in the life of a true believer, no one who has these symptoms has any right to assume that he is a true believer because he has these symptoms. A person might as well conclude that he is a believer because he is an adulterer because David, who was a true believer, was once an adulterer. Only a fool would argue:

A wise man may be sick and wounded, yes, even do some foolish things; therefore, everyone who is sick and wounded and does some foolish things is a wise man.

No, he that has such symptoms may only safely conclude, 'If I am a believer, I am a most miserable one.' And if such a person is a true believer he can expect no real peace as long as he remains content in such a state.

10.
The second particular rule for mortification

In the previous chapter we dealt with a rule that was preparatory to the duty of mortification. Before any mortification can be carried out there must be a careful diagnosis of the sinful desire to be mortified. Have you done this? Once this has been done, and only then, are we ready to move on to the second particular rule for mortification. It is this:

Strive to fill your mind and conscience with a clear and constant awareness of the guilt, the danger and the evil of the sinful desire that is troubling you.

1) The guilt of your sinful desire.
The believer must refuse to be deceived by the deceitful reasonings of his sinful desire. It will always try to excuse and lessen its own guilt. It is always ready to reason like this:

'Maybe this is bad, yet there are things far worse! Other saints have not merely thought these things, they have done them...'

In a hundred different ways sin will seek to divert the mind from a correct understanding of its guilt. As the prophet tells us:

'prostitution, to old wine and to new, which take away the understanding.' (Hosea 4:11).

In the same way that these sinful desires fully succeed in doing this to the non-Christian, so to a certain extent they will succeed in doing this to the Christian.

In Proverbs we are given a sad picture of a young man who was enticed by a prostitute. This youth lacked 'understanding' (Proverbs 7:7). What exactly was the 'understanding' he lacked? The answer is that he didn't know that giving into his lust would 'cost him his life' (Proverbs 7:23) - he did not consider the guilt of the evil he was involved in.

If we want to mortify sin we must fully realise that it will seek to dim our awareness of its guilt. Then we must aim to fix a right understanding of its guilt in our minds. There are two things we should think about to assist us in this:

a) **A believer's sin is far greater than an unbeliever's.** The grace of God at work in a believer will weaken the power of sin so that it is no longer his master as it is the master of others (see Romans 6:14,16). At the same time, however, the guilt of sin that remains in a believer is made worse by the fact that the believer sins against grace!

'What shall we say, then? Shall we go on sinning, so that grace may increase? By no means! We died to sin; how can we live in it any longer?' (Romans 6: 1,2).

In this text the emphasis is on the word 'we'. How shall **we** do it? Doubtless, we are more evil; than any if we do. We sin against the love of God. We sin against the mercy of God. We sin in spite of promises of assistance to defeat sin. Much more could be said, but let this final consideration be impressed upon your minds:

*In every believer's heart there is far more evil and guilt in
the sin that remains there, than there would be in that same
measure of sin in a graceless heart.*

b) **Think about how God views your sin.**

When God sees the longings after holiness that grace has
produced in the heart of any of his servants he sees more beauty
and excellence in them that he sees in the most glorious works
of men devoid of grace. Yes, God even sees more beauty and
excellence in these inner longings than he sees in most of their
outward acts. This is because there is nearly always a greater
mixture of sin in an outward act than in the desires and longings
after holiness of a gracious heart.

On the other hand, God sees a great deal of evil in the sinful
desire of a believer. God sees more evil in that sinful desire
than he sees in the open, notorious acts of wicked men. He even
sees more evil in that than he does in many of the outward sins
that saints may fall into. Why is this? It is because God sees that
there is more inward opposition made against sin itself, and
generally there is more humiliation over the sin. This is why
Christ deals with spiritual decay in his children by going to the
root and exposing their true state. 'I know...' (Revelation
3:15).

Reader, you must seek to let these and other similar considerations lead you to a clear awareness of the guilt of your
indwelling sinful desire. Don't underestimate or try to excuse
your guilt in this or else your sinful desire will get strength and
prevail without your being aware of it.

2) **The danger of your sinful desire.**

There are many dangers to be considered but we will confine
our thoughts to four of them:

a) **The danger of being hardened.** Consider the warnings
of Hebrews 3:12,13. In these words the writer solemnly
charges his readers to do all in their power to avoid being

'hardened by sin's deceitfulness'. The hardening mentioned here is total apostasy, a hardening that turns a person 'away from the living God'. Any sinful desire left unmortified tends to such hardening and makes at least some progress towards it. The person reading these words may once have been very tender towards God and often found their heart moved by his Word. But now, alas, things have changed and you can pass over duties of prayer, reading and hearing God's Word with little concern. It is not enough to make your heart tremble to think of it becoming so hard that you think lightly of sin, the wonder of God's grace, God's mercy, the precious blood of Christ, the law of God, heaven and hell. Reader, take care. This is what unmortified sinful desire will do if left unchecked.

b) **The danger of some great temporal punishment.**
Although God will never utterly forsake any of his children for failing to mortify their sinful desire, he may chasten them, causing them pain and sorrow (see Psalm 89:30-33). Think of David and all the troubles he had because he failed to mortify his sinful desire for Bathsheba. Is it nothing to you that your failure to mortify sinful desires in your life may bring upon you painful chastisements that may continue with you to the grave? If you have no fear of such a thing then you have good cause to fear your heart has been hardened.

c) **The danger of loss of peace and strength for a lifetime.**
Peace with God and strength to walk before God are essential to the spiritual life of the soul. Without enjoying these things in some measure, to live is to die. When a person persists in leaving his sinful desire unmortified, sooner or later he will be deprived of both these blessings. What peace or strength can a soul enjoy when God says, 'I was enraged by his sinful greed; I punished him, and hid my face in anger' (as he did in Isaiah 57:17)? Elsewhere God says, 'Then I will go back to my place until they admit their guilt' (Hosea 5:15). And, when God does that, what will become of their peace and strength?

Think, reader, could it be, perhaps, that in a very little while you will see the face of God in peace no more? Perhaps by tomorrow you will not be able to pray, read, hear or perform any duties with the least cheerfulness, life or vigour. Perhaps God will shoot his arrows at you and fill you with anguish, with fears and perplexities. Consider this for a while, even though God will not utterly destroy you, yet he might cast you into a state where you feel that this is what will happen to you. Don't leave this consideration until your soul trembles within you.

d) **The danger of eternal destruction** [Owen makes two observations concerning this danger, but we shall confine ourselves to the first of these.]

There is such a connection between a persistence in sin and eternal destruction that as long as a person is under the power of sin they must be warned about destruction and everlasting separation from God. The fact that God has resolved to deliver some from a continuance in sin (in order to save them from destruction) doesn't change the other (equally true) fact that God will deliver none from destruction that continue in sin. God's rule is very clear. 'A man reaps what he sows. The one who sows to please his sinful nature, from that nature will reap destruction...' (Galatians 6:7,8). The more clearly we recognise the reality that unmortified sinful desire will lead to eternal destruction, the more clearly we will see the danger of allowing any sinful desire in our life to remain unmortified. Sinful desire is an enemy that will destroy us if we don't destroy it first. Let this sink deep into your soul. Don't be content that it has sunk deep enough till your soul trembles at the thought of having an enemy living within you that will destroy you unless you destroy it first.

3) The evils of your lust.

Danger is concerned with future possibilities but evil is concerned with the present. There are many evils connected with an unmortified sinful desire but we will focus our attention on only three of them:

a) **It grieves the holy and blessed Spirit of God.** It is the great privilege of believers that the Spirit of God lives within them. Because of this, believers are especially exhorted in Ephesians 4:25-29 to abstain from a variety of sinful desires and motivated to do so by the words,

'do not grieve the Holy Spirit of God, with whom you were sealed for the day of redemption' (Ephesians 4:30).

Just as a tender and loving person is grieved by the unkindness of a friend so the Holy Spirit is grieved when a believer allows unmortified sinful desires to live in his heart. The Holy Spirit has chosen our hearts as his home. He has come to do for us all the good we desire. How the Holy Spirit is grieved when a believer shares the heart he has come to possess with his enemies (our sinful desires), the very enemies he has come to help destroy.

Oh, believer, consider who and what you are; who the Spirit is who is grieved, what he has done for you and what he intends to do for you. Be ashamed of every unmortified sinful desire you allow to defile his temple.

b) **The Lord Jesus Christ is wounded afresh by it.** When sinful desire remains unmortified in a believer's heart, Christ's new creation in that heart is wounded, his love is frustrated, his enemy gratified. Just as a total abandoning of Christ by the deceitfulness of sin is, 'crucifying the Son of God all over again, and subjecting him to public disgrace' (Hebrews 6:6), so harbouring of every sin that he came to destroy, wounds and grieves him.

c) **It takes away a believer's usefulness.** Unmortified sinful desire usually produces a spiritual disease in a person's life. Their witness seldom receives blessing from God. Many believers allow soul-destroying sinful desires to live in their hearts. These lie like worms at the root of their obedience, and corrode and weaken it day by day. All graces, all the ways and means whereby any graces may be exercised and improved, are hindered in this way; and God himself denies this man any success.

Conclusion:

Never forget the guilt, danger and evil of sin. Think much on these things. Let them fill your mind until they cause your heart to tremble.

11.
Five more particular rules for mortification

Rule 3: Disturb your conscience with the guilt of your evil desire. What does this mean and how can it be done? It means that you must do more than merely recognise the guilt of your evil desire. You must disturb your conscience with the guilt of your own particular evil desire. How can you do this? Let us think about two general and two specific ways.

1) Two general ways:

a) **Expose your conscience to the searching light of God's law.**
Pray for the convicting work of the Holy Spirit; that he would use the law of God to convince you of the greatness of your guilt. Let the terror of God's law sink into your conscience. Think of how righteous God would be if he punished every one of your transgressions of his law. Don't allow your deceitful heart to argue that God's law cannot condemn you because you 'are not under law but under grace' (Romans 6:14).

Tell your conscience that as long as unmortified evil desire remains in your heart you can have no valid assurance that you are free from its condemning power. God has given the law to condemn sin wherever it is found. God's law is meant to expose the guilt of a believer's sin just as much as any other person's sin. God's law is meant to awaken believers to the guilt of their sin so that they might humble themselves and deal with it. To be unwilling to let God's law disturb your conscience is not a good sign. Rather it is a sad indication of the hardness of your heart and the deceitfulness of sin.

Beware of thinking that deliverance from the penalty of God's law means that it is no longer meant to direct your life or expose your sin. This is a dangerous error that has ruined many a professing Christian. If you claim to be the Lord's, refuse to think that way. Rather, persuade your conscience to listen carefully to what God's law says about your sinful desires and sinful ways. Oh! if you do this, it will make you tremble and bring you to your knees. If you really want to put to death your sinful desires, let the law of God disturb your conscience until you are convinced of the awful guilt of your sinful desires. Don't be content before you can say with repentant David, 'I know my transgressions, and my sin is always before me' (Psalm 51:3).

b) **Let the gospel condemn and put to death your sinful desires.**

Think about all you owe the gospel. Say to yourself, 'God has shown me such grace, love and mercy and what have I done? I've despised and trampled on his goodness to me. Is this how I show my appreciation of a Father's love and the blood of his Son? How could I defile the heart that Christ died to cleanse, that God's blessed Spirit came to dwell in? What can I say to my dear Lord Jesus? Is my fellowship with him of so little value that I can let my heart be so filled with sinful desires that there is almost no room left for him? How can I daily 'grieve the Spirit who has sealed me for the day of redemption (Ephesians 4:30)?' Consider these things every day and, with the Holy Spirit's help, you will be disgusted with the vileness of your sinful desires and you will want to put them to death.

2) Two specific ways:

a) Think about God's infinite patience and longsuffering to you.

Think how easily God could have exposed you to the shame and reproach of this world. Yet in his mercy he has kept your sin from the eyes of the world and often restrained you from open sin. How easily God could have brought your sinful life to an end and sent you to hell. In spite of all his goodness to you in these ways, you have continued to let your sinful desires have their way. How often you have provoked God by refusing to make any effort or by making very little effort to put your sinful desires to death. Are you going to go on wearying God and trying his patience?

Think of times when you have wilfully planned ways to gratify the desires of your sinful nature and God has graciously thwarted you. Think of times when you have given in so much to your sinful desires that your conscience has alarmed you and made you fear that God can no longer have mercy on you. And yet, God has had mercy upon you and brought you to fresh repentance and faith.

b) Think about God's repeated gracious dealings with you.

Think how often God's mercy has saved you from being hardened by the deceitfulness of sin. Think about the many times you have found your spiritual life grown cold; times when your delight in God's ways, in prayer, in meditation upon God's Word and fellowship with God's people have almost vanished. Think of times when in various ways you have wandered from God and yet God has rescued and restored you.

Think of the many amazing providences God has brought into your life. Think of the trials he has made to become a blessing to you and the trials he has spared you. Think of every way God has blessed you. After all these displays of God's grace to you, can you continue to allow sinful desires that will harden your heart against such grace? Disturb your conscience with the help of such thoughts and don't stop until your heart is deeply affected by your guilt. Until this happens you will never make vigorous efforts to put these sinful desires to death. Until this is done there will be no powerful motive to move on and work at the fourth rule.

Rule 4: Strive to develop a constant longing for deliverance from the power of your sinful desires.

The longing for deliverance is a grace in itself and has power to help you achieve what you long for. For example, when the Apostle Paul describes the repentance and godly sorrow of the Corinthians he uses the expression 'vehement desire' (cf. 'what longing' 2 Corinthians 7:11). You can be certain that unless you long for deliverance you will never get it. Strong desire is the essence of true prayer. Strong desire will set your faith and hope in God's deliverance. Keep crying to God for this grace of constant longing until your deliverance comes!

Rule 5: Learn to recognise that some of your sinful desires are rooted in your very nature.

A tendency to certain sins is rooted in your sinful nature. For example, some people have much greater difficulty controlling their temper than others. Some people have a natural tendency to eat too much or to laziness or some other sinful behaviour. This means that you need to know the sinful tendencies that are rooted in your nature. These tendencies are not to be excused as, 'that is just my nature'. No, you are to recognise the guilt of having these sinful tendencies and strive to overcome them.

One remedy that ought to be applied to counteract such sinful tendencies is the one which the Apostle Paul used in 1 Corinthians 9:27: 'I beat my body and make it my slave.' In other words, you bring your bodily appetites under control, with God's help, by means of prayer and sometimes fasting.

This is not to be confused with the 'harsh treatment of the body' condemned by the same apostle in Colossians 2:23. No, this is a voluntary humbling of your soul using the God-appointed means of fasting and looking to the Spirit of God to bless it, in weakening sinful desires that are rooted in your nature.

Rule 6: Watch and guard your soul against everything you know that could encourage your sinful desires.
This duty will be explained more fully in the other part of this book that deals with temptation. At this point we simply notice the words of King David: 'I keep myself from my iniquity' (Psalm 18:23). David watched all the ways and workings of his sinful desires, to prevent them and fight against them. You must do the same. This means that you must think about the circumstances that usually encourage your sinful desires and do all you can to avoid such circumstances. For example, if you know that in certain company your sinful desires are encouraged, you must try to avoid that company. Or, if duty demands that you mix with these people, you must be specially watchful.

If you suffer from an illness it is your wisdom to avoid anything which you know will make it worse. Now if you take such care of your physical health, how much more should you do the same for your spiritual health. Remember, he who dares to play with opportunities to sin will dare to sin. The way to avoid adultery with a prostitute is, 'Keep to a path far from her, do not go near the door of her house...' (Proverbs 5:8).

Rule 7: Fight your sinful desires as soon as they start.
If you saw a spark fly out of the fire on to a carpet you would stamp it out right away, You would not give it the chance to set your carpet on fire and burn your house down. Treat sinful desires in the same way. Consider what an unclean thought can lead to. If it is left unchecked, sooner or later, unclean acts will follow. Ask envy where it wants to go. Be assured that envy left

unchecked will, sooner or later, end in murder and destruction. If you don't check sin at its very start, it's unlikely that you will be able to check it later. Give sin an inch and it will try to take a mile. It is impossible to fix bounds on sin. It is like water in a channel - if it once breaks out, it will have its course (see Proverbs 17:14).

12.
Meditating upon the excellent majesty of God

Rule 8: Meditate upon the excellent majesty of God.
This is the way to humble yourself and see how vile you are.
When Job really saw the greatness and excellency of God he
confessed, 'I despise myself, and repent in dust and ashes' (Job
42:5,6,). Scripture shows us many similar examples of godly
men (e.g. Isaiah, Daniel, Peter and John) being greatly humbled and overwhelmed when God revealed something of his
greatness and excellence. If you take seriously the way God's
Word compares the men of this world to 'grasshoppers', to
'worthless', the 'dust on the scales' (see Isaiah 40:12-25) when
compared to God, it will do much to keep you humble. A truly
humble spirit will greatly help your efforts to put your sinful
desires to death. The more you meditate upon the greatness of
God the more you will feel the vileness of your sinful desires.
   One way of helping you meditate upon the greatness of God
is simply to recognise how little of God you really know. You
can know enough of God to keep you humble but when you add
up everything you know about God you still know very little.
It was thinking like this that made the wise man Agur realise
how 'ignorant' ('brutish', A.V. Proverbs 30:1-4) he was. The
more you come to realise just how little you know of God, the
more the pride of your heart will be humbled.

Begin to think about your ignorance of God by thinking how ignorant even the godliest of men are in their knowledge of God. Think of Moses who pleaded with God, 'show me your glory' (Exodus 33:18). God showed him some most glorious things about himself (see Exodus 34:5-7) but these things were only the 'back' of God, because God said, 'You cannot see my face, for no one may see me and live' (Exodus 33:20). Some people may think that since Jesus Christ came our knowledge of God has grown much greater than Moses' knowledge. There is some truth in this, but it is equally true that, in spite of the revelation of God given in Jesus Christ, the godliest of believers still only see the 'back' of God.

The Apostle Paul, who probably saw the glory of God more clearly than anyone (2 Corinthians 3:18), could only see it by means of a mirror. Think about what Paul writes in 1 Corinthians 13:12, 'Now we see but a poor reflection... Now I know in part.' Paul compares all his present knowledge of God with the kind of knowledge he had when he was a child (1 Corinthians 13:12). You may love, honour, believe and obey your heavenly Father and he will accept your childish thoughts; but that is what they are, childish. However much we have learned of him, we still know very little. One day we will know so much more that we can possibly know now, but for the present even those who see the glory of God most clearly can only see it dimly.

When the Queen of Sheba, who had heard so much about the greatness of King Solomon, eventually saw this greatness with her own eyes she had to confess, 'not even half was told me' (1 Kings 10:7). We may imagine our knowledge of God is good but when we are brought into his presence we shall cry out, 'We never knew him as he is; the thousandth part of his glory and perfection and blessedness, never entered into our hearts.'

Many of the things that we believe are true of God, we simply don't understand. We cannot understand an invisible

God. Who can understand the description given to us in 1 Timothy 6:16, 'Who alone is immortal and who lives in unapproachable light, whom no one has seen or can see'? The glory of God is so great that no creature can look upon it and live. God describes himself to us in these ways to help us see just how different he is from us, to show us just how little we can know him as he really is.

Think of the eternity of God: a God with no beginning and no ending. We can believe this, but who can understand eternity? The same is true of the mystery of the Trinity. How can God be One and yet Three; only one God yet three distinct Persons in the same undivided essence? No one can understand this. That is the reason why many refuse to believe it. By faith we can believe the mystery of the Trinity, but no believer really understands it.

Not only do we understand so little about the being of God, we also understand so little about his ways. God says, 'my thoughts are not your thoughts, neither are your ways my ways...as the heavens are higher than the earth, so are my ways higher than your ways, and my thoughts than your thoughts' (Isaiah 55:8,9). The apostle Paul writes something very similar to the Romans: 'Oh, the depth of the riches both of the wisdom and knowledge of God! How unsearchable are his judgements and his ways past finding out!' (Romans 11:33). Although sometimes the Lord shows us reasons for the things he does, there are many times when we simply cannot understand God's ways.

In seeking to stress how little the believer knows of God we are not suggesting God is unknowable. We are not underestimating the tremendous revelation God has given of himself through his Son. In many different ways God has revealed a great deal of himself. The point we are making is simply that we are incapable of fully understanding even what he has revealed. We must be thankful for all we can know of God, but the more we know the more we are humbled by how little we really know.

There are two things we must never forget:

One: We must never forget God's purpose in what he reveals of himself. It is given not to unveil God's essential glory so that we see him as he is. Rather, he simply gives enough knowledge of himself for us to have faith in him, to trust, love and obey him. This is as much knowledge of God as it is suitable for us to have in this present state. However, in the future state he will make a new revelation of himself to us so that all we know now will seem but a shadow of the fuller revelation he gives then.

Two: We must never forget how dull and slow of heart we are to receive all that the Word of God would teach us about God. In spite of the clear revelation God has given we still know so little of what he has revealed.

As you think of what you know about God and how little you know this great God, pray that this will be a means to humble you. May God himself continually fill your soul with a holy and awesome fear of him so that sinful desires can never thrive or flourish in your soul.

13.
Don't let your heart deceive you!

Rule 9: Guard against the deceitfulness of your heart.
God's Word clearly tells us, 'The heart is deceitful above all things' (Jeremiah 17:9) and many a bitter experience confirms this. With this ninth rule we are thinking of a particular form of self-deception. We are thinking about how a false peace can deceive us. The rule for preventing such a false peace can be put like this:

Be careful you don't speak peace to yourself before God does.
Your conscience is the voice of God: listen to what it says. When you sin, or when you are made aware of the power of some sinful desire, your conscience will trouble you. This is God's way of warning you of danger. It is God disturbing your peace. It is God troubling your soul so that you turn to him and ask him to communicate his peace to your soul. When God troubles you like this, your greatest danger is to speak a false peace to your soul. In Jeremiah's day the false prophets were guilty of proclaiming such a false peace. This is how God speaks of them, 'They dress the wound of my people as though it were not serious. 'Peace, peace,' they say, when there is no peace' (Jeremiah 6:14). You must be careful you don't speak like a false prophet to your own soul and say, 'Peace, peace' when God has not given that peace.

Five ways to know the difference between the peace that God gives and the false peace you can give yourself.

1) Any peace that does not bring with it a hatred of the sin that has disturbed your peace is false.

The peace that God speaks to the soul always brings with it a sense of shame and a holy desire to put your sinful desires to death. If you look upon Christ whom your sin has pierced (unless you do this there is neither healing nor peace) you will 'mourn' (Zechariah 12:10). When you go to Christ for healing, your faith rests upon a pierced and wounded Saviour. Now, if you do this in the strength of the Holy Spirit, you will be given a hatred for the sin which has disturbed your peace. When God speaks peace the soul is filled with shame for all the ways that sin has spoiled our peace with God (Ezekiel 16:59-63).

It is possible to be troubled by the consequences of sin without hating the sin itself. In your trouble you can be seeking mercy from Jesus Christ yet at the same time holding on to the sin you love. Such seeking of mercy will never bring true solid peace. For example, your conscience convicts you of loving the world. God's words, 'If anyone loves the world, the love of the Father is not in him' (1 John 2:15) disturb your peace. In your trouble you turn to God to heal your soul but you are more troubled about the consequences of your love of the world than you are about the evil of that love. This is a bad sign! Perhaps you will be saved; but unless God has special dealings that make you really hate your sin, you will have little peace in this life.

2) Any peace that is not accompanied by the Spirit's convincing of 'sin and righteousness and judgement' is a false peace.

God's word of peace never comes in 'word only', it comes in the power of the Holy Spirit. God's peace actually heals the wound. When we speak a false peace to ourselves it won't be

136

long before the sin that disturbed our peace has broken out again.

As a general rule God expects his children to wait until they are sure he has communicated peace to them. As the prophet Isaiah says, 'I will wait for the Lord, who is hiding his face from the house of Jacob' (Isaiah 8:17). God can heal the wound of sin is an instant. However, sometimes, like a doctor, he takes time to clean the wound thoroughly so that it heals properly. Those who speak a false peace to themselves never have time to wait for God to do his thorough work. Such a person rushes to God for peace and assumes he has received it the moment he asked for it. There is no waiting for the Spirit of God to heal the wound of sin thoroughly.

God's peace sweetens the heart and gives joy to the soul. When God speaks peace, his words are not just true. They do good to the soul. 'Do not my words do good?' (Micah 2:7). When God speaks peace, it guides and keeps the soul so that it will not return to folly (Psalm 85:8). When people speak peace to themselves, the heart is not healed of the evil and they continue in a state of backsliding. When Gods speaks peace, there comes with it such an awareness of his love that the soul feels obliged to put to death sinful desires.

3) Any peace that deals with sin in a superficial way is a false peace.

As we noted earlier, this is the complaint Jeremiah made of the false prophets of his day. '"Peace, peace," they say, when there is no peace.' (Jeremiah 6:14). In the same way, some people make the healing of their sinful wounds an easy work. They look at some promise in the Scripture and they think they are healed. A promise of Scripture can only do good when it is mixed with faith (Hebrews 4:2). It is not a mere look at the word of mercy in the promise that brings peace. The look must be mixed with faith until you have made the promise your own. Otherwise any peace you get from it is a false peace. In such a case it won't be long before your wound opens again and you will know it is not yet cured.

4) Any peace that deals with sin in a partial way is false.
The sincere believer will not simply seek to be at peace from more troublesome sinful desires. To seek to deal with sin that bothers us and not to deal with those that trouble us less is to deal with sin partially. Any peace that seems to come from dealing with sin like this is false. We can only expect God's peace when we have an equal respect to all his commandments. God justifies us from all our sins. God commands us to get rid of all our sins. He is a God of purer eyes than to behold iniquity.

5) God's peace is a humbling peace, as it was in the case of David (see Psalm 51:1).
Think of the deep humiliation felt by David when Nathan brought him God's word of pardon (2 Samuel 12:13).

To sum up: If you wish to be sure of God's peace being spoken to you, learn to walk closely with your Saviour. Jesus tells us, 'my sheep hear my voice.' As we learn to commune with our Saviour we will learn to distinguish between his voice and the voice of a stranger. When he speaks, he speaks like no other man, he speaks with power. When Jesus speaks, in one way or another, he will make your heart burn within you as he did with the disciples on the Emmaus road (Luke 24).

The other major evidence of the Lord speaking peace to the soul is the good that it does. We know the Lord has spoken peace when the result is a humbler person. We know the Lord has spoken peace when our sinful desires are actually weakened. When the promises of peace make you love the Lord and purify your soul, when they humble your heart in true sorrow for sin, when they urge you to loving obedience and rid the soul of self-love, then the Lord has spoken peace.

14.
Final instructions

From chapter nine we have been thinking about how to prepare your heart for the work of putting your sinful desires to death. In this final chapter we concentrate upon the work itself. There are two aspects to this work:

1) The actual work the believer is responsible to perform.
2) The work that only the Spirit of God can perform.

1) The actual work the believer is responsible to perform.
This can be summed up as the believer's active faith in Christ's power and authority to kill his sin. To be specific, faith must believe in the blood of Christ as the only effective remedy for sin-sick souls. If you constantly set your faith in this effective remedy you will die a conqueror. More than that, through the providence of God you will live to see your sinful desires dead at your feet.

a) Some instructions for the exercise of this faith:
    i) **Confident faith and trust in Christ will provide everything you need to kill your sinful desire.** Focus your faith upon this wonderful truth and continually meditate upon it. On the one hand it is true that in your own strength you will

never conquer these powerful sinful desires. You may have tried and failed so often that you are weary with the battle and ready to give up. Yet you must focus your faith on the one who has the power to enable you to triumph in his strength. You can enter into the confident claim of the Apostle Paul, 'I can do all things through Christ who strengthens me.' (Philippians 4:13 NKJV). However powerful and ungovernable your sinful desires may be, focus you mind on the fullness of the grace of Christ. Fix your mind upon the treasures of strength, might and help that are in Christ for your support (see John 1:16; Colossians 1:19). Let such thoughts constantly fill your mind.

Think of Jesus as the One who is exalted and made a Prince and Saviour to give repentance to Israel (Acts 5:31). The repentance he gives includes the grace of mortification (i.e. the power to subdue your sinful desires and put them to death). Again, think on the grace that Christ gives as the believer abides in him (John 15:1-5).

Let your faith live on thoughts like the following: 'I am a poor, weak, unstable creature. My sinful desires are too strong for me. I'm in danger of being ruined by them and I don't know what to do. I have broken all my resolves and promises to put my sinful desires to death. I know from bitter experience that I do not have the strength to conquer them. I can see that without God's mighty help I'll be lost. I look to the Lord Jesus Christ and see in him a fullness of grace and power to put to death these enemies of mine. I see in Christ a provision sufficient to make me conquer all my inward enemies (i.e. sinful desires).'

Meditate on passages like Isaiah 35:1-7 and 40:27-31. Believe with the Apostle Paul that there is sufficient grace to put to death every sinful desire (2 Corinthians 12:9).

Even though you don't enjoy the victory in every conflict, continue to trust in the resources of Christ to give you the ultimate victory.

ii) **Encourage your heart by faith to expect Christ's help.** This instruction takes us a stage further than the first one. It moves us from simply believing that Christ can help us to believe that he will. Faith goes on to hope for actual deliverance. Faith waits upon the Lord to come and help. Even though the Lord's deliverance seems slow to come, faith continues to wait for it.

b) Some thoughts to promote an expentant faith in your hearts:

i) **Think much upon Christ as your great High Priest in heaven.** Think about his merciful, tender, kindly nature. Be assured that he pities you in your distress. Remember that your great High Priest has the tenderness of a mother to her infant child (Isaiah 66:13). Remember the great purpose of Jesus in taking our human nature. 'In all things he had to be made like his brethren, that he might be a merciful and faithful high priest in things pertaining to God, to make propitiation for the sins of the people. For that he himself has suffered, being tempted, he is able to aid those who are tempted' (Hebrews 2:17,18). Hold on to the wonderful promise of Hebrews 4:15,16. You need spiritual help, and God has his Son seated upon a 'throne of grace'. God invites you to come boldly to that throne of grace that you may obtain mercy and find grace to help in time of need.

ii) **Think much about the faithfulness of the promises of God.** God has made promises that you can rely on. God tells us that his covenant with us is like the sun, moon and stars which have their certain courses (Jeremiah 31: 35,36). Fix your hope on specific promises concerning the purpose of Christ's work. For example 'Jesus 'will save his people from their sins' (Matthew 1:21). 'The Son of God was manifested, that he might destroy the works of the devil' (1 John 3:8). Be certain that these promises cannot fail. You can rely upon the faithfulness of God.

iii) **Meditate on the advantages which will always be gained from expecting help to come from Jesus Christ.** There are two such advantages:

a) **By expecting such help we actually honour Christ by our confidence in him and our dependence upon him.** Whenever a believer honours Christ in this way he can be certain that his faith in Christ will not be disappointed. The Psalmist tells us, 'Those who know your name will trust in you, for you, LORD, have never forsaken those who seek you' (Psalm 9:10). You can be certain that if your trust is placed in Christ he won't fail you.

b) **If we really expect such help to come from Christ we will use every means that will bring us this help.** If you were a beggar and you believed a certain man could give you help, you would do all you could to bring your need to the notice of this man. If he promises help and tells you how he will help you, then you will do what he tells you. In the same way, (e.g. prayer, meditation on the Word of God, fellowship with God's people, etc.), you will use these means.

iv) **Focus your faith especially upon the death of Christ.** The fundamental reason for putting to death your sinful desires is the death of Christ. The great aim of the death of Christ was to destroy the works of the devil. 'Who gave himself for us, to redeem us from all iniquity, and to purify for himself a people that are his very own, eager to do what is good' (Titus 2:14). He died to free us from the power of our sins and to purify us from every sinful desire that defiles us.

Focus your faith on Christ as he is set forth in the gospel as dying and crucified for us. Look on him as he prays, bleeds and dies under the weight of your sin. By faith bring this crucified Saviour to live in your heart (Ephesians 3:17). By faith apply his blood to all your sinful desires. Make this a daily practice.

2) The work that only the Spirit can perform.

The work of putting sin to death is only possible and can only be accomplished in the power of the Holy Spirit. Unless the Holy Spirit gives us strength we will work in vain. Let us consider what the Spirit does to make our work successful.

a) He alone can clearly and fully convince your heart of the evil, guilt and danger of its sinful desires. Until this work of his is done, you will make no progress in putting your sinful desires to death. This is the first thing that the Spirit does; he convinces the soul of all the evil, guilt and danger of every sinful desire. The Holy Spirit works until the heart confesses its evil and longs for deliverance. Unless the Spirit does this great work, none of the other works that follow can be done.

b) The Spirit is able to reveal to you the fullness of Christ to meet your need. Until the Spirit does this you will have nothing to keep your heart from seeking a false way of dealing with your sin or being driven to despair and despondency (see 2 Corinthians 2:7,8).

c) The Spirit alone is able to assure you that Christ will come to help you, and to enable you to wait patiently in faith until he does.

d) It is by the Spirit that we are baptised into the death of Christ. It was he alone who brought the cross of Christ into your heart with all its sin-killing power. It is he alone who continues to apply this powerful remedy.

e) The Spirit is the author and finisher of your sanctification. It is the Spirit who gives new supplies and influences of grace for holiness and sanctification as he weakens the power of your sinful desires.

f) The Spirit supports you continually as you seek God's help to overcome your sinful desires. He is the 'Spirit of supplication' promised to those who look on 'the one they have pierced' (Zechariah 12:10). He 'himself intercedes for us with groans that words cannot express' (Romans 8:26).